THE EVERYDAY VISIONARY

Focus Your Thoughts, Change Your Life

JESSE DUPLANTIS

A TOUCHSTONE / HOWARD BOOK
PUBLISHED BY SIMON & SCHUSTER
NEW YORK   LONDON   TORONTO   SYDNEY

Touchstone/Howard Books
A Division of Simon & Schuster, Inc.
1230 Avenue of the Americas
HOWARD New York, NY 10020

First Touchstone/Howard Books hardcover edition July 2008

TOUCHSTONE/HOWARD BOOKS and colophon are registered trademarks of Simon & Schuster, Inc.

For information about special discounts for bulk purchases, please contact Simon & Schuster Special Sales at 1-800-456-6798 or business@simonandschuster.com

Designed by Mary Austin Speaker

Manufactured in the United States of America

10   9   8   7   6

Library of Congress Cataloging-in-Publication Data

Duplantis, Jesse.
    The everyday visionary : focus your thoughts,
change your life / Jesse Duplantis.
        p. cm.
    "A Touchstone/Howard book."
1. Spirituality. 2. Christian life. I. Title.
BV4501.3.D87 2007
248.4—dc22   2007033602

ISBN-13: 978-1-4165-4976-5
ISBN-10:   1-4165-4976-5

This book is dedicated to my wife, Cathy, who put up with me when I couldn't put up with myself! I love you, Cathy!

CONTENTS

CONTENTS

THE EVERYDAY VISIONARY

CHAPTER I

BUILDING MENTAL MAPS TO DESTINY

DREAMING IS WONDERFUL. Doing is better. When I first began in ministry, the Lord told me that I was going to be preaching the Gospel on worldwide television one day. Now, at that time, that looked about as possible as seeing a pig fly over south Louisiana. I barely had enough money for gas to fill up my car. I felt blessed to preach in a church that sat fifty people. And, I sure didn't think that, with my accent and my Cajun heritage, that anyone would want to listen to me preach the Gospel on TV.

Still, I knew the voice of the Lord. My life had been completely turned around through another man's television ministry and I knew that God would use me to reach others through the same vehicle.

I grew up along the banks of the Mississippi River, in south Louisiana. I learned early that nobody was going to take care of me, but me. I saw a lot of poverty and a lot of hypocrisy. I experienced hardship from a young age and I had a pretty bad view of the church in general, but my mother was a strong believer and a strong woman, and she instilled the Scriptures in me from the time I was a young boy. Still, I didn't believe it and I just wanted to get out.

So, although I made my own choices and used my musical talent to get out of Louisiana and play rock music as a young man, when I came back around and gave my life to God, I knew that it meant change . . . change not only in my spirit and in my heart, but also in my mind.

MENTAL CHANGES, MENTAL CHOICES

When I decided to follow the teachings of Jesus and the Bible, it was also a decision to change my mental strategies. Before, I didn't understand spiritual concepts like faith. But after I accepted Christ and chose to go this way in my life, I began to get a clearer picture of what it meant to think God's way, to trust Him and start living by the teachings in His Word.

Years later, after I accepted God's call on my life and entered the ministry, God dropped the idea of preaching the Word on worldwide television into my mind. It was a big thought and, I knew, totally beyond my means.

It could have easily stayed in the realm of dreaming, but I decided to move that thought out of idleness into the realm of real faith. To even begin doing that, I had to "reboot" my mind, so to speak, and actually consider that the dream *could* come to pass. After all, everything around me told me that I couldn't do it. But, I knew that this was a "God-thought"—a thought that was not about me, but about reaching more people for Him.

That day, I began developing a "mental map"—a determined thought-life—that I knew would be a key in reaching what I believed God had told me would be part of my destiny. I knew that this thought wasn't a pipe dream. It wasn't a thought that I wanted to dismiss with a "well, maybe one day" kind of attitude. I knew in my heart that I needed to go deeper with the idea that I considered to be "God-revealed."

MENTAL MAPS ARE DETERMINED THOUGHTS

You see, daydreams are idle thoughts. They can be fun. They can be a form of escape. But mental maps are the kind of thoughts that have purpose and direction. They're the thoughts with intent, thoughts that are actually taking you somewhere that you want to go. You could call them "determined" thoughts.

You know the difference. Think about it. Have you ever been watching TV and a commercial for cake mix comes on the screen? Shot one, you're suddenly seeing close-ups of a butter-yellow cake with chocolate icing. The announcer is telling you how good it is as, shot two, that steaming cake comes sliding out of the oven.

Shot three, you watch a fork press down on the top of the cake and the cake just fluffs right back up, like the freshest thing ever made. Shot four, they get a tight angle on a knife sliding across the top of that cake with chocolate frosting so thick and so close that you can almost reach out and grab it.

Shot five, a big old slice of that cake sits on a plate as another fork cuts right down and lifts up quick to take the first bite—the act of the fork coming up quick creates a perfect little twirl of chocolate icing. It looks like it's just waiting for that fork to come in and make that next bite . . . which the fork never does. Instead, the camera zooms in closer and closer to the cake. The name brand of the mix comes on the screen and it's all over. The TV is rolling on to something else.

Okay, now, here's where thoughts come in. You've just seen the commercial. You start wanting that cake. You sit there for a second and imagine tasting yellow cake with chocolate icing. It's just an idle thought, a passing thought.

A "determined" thought is different. It has intent and passion behind it. A determined thought isn't content to remain idle, it gives you an idea!

In this case, a determined thought gives you the idea of preheating the oven. Then, it is this kind of thought that actually gets your rear off the sofa at ten at night! It's the kind of thought that has you speeding to the grocery store to get that mix, the kind of thought that has you reading the back of the box in your kitchen and going through all the steps it takes to have that cake mixed, baked, and frosted, so that you can sit right back down where you were before in front of the

TV . . . except with a hot slice of cake on a plate in your hand and a big smile of accomplishment on your face! My wife and I do this kind of thing once every few years. I know what I'm talking about!

Now, do you see the difference? An idle thought keeps you on the couch. A determined thought gets you inspired to *move*.

FROM MENTAL MAPS TO REALITY

Here's how it goes. A mental map begins with determined thoughts. Those determined thoughts produce ideas. Those ideas produce actions. And those actions—combined with faith in God, trust in His Word, and the tenacity to never give up—are what will draw your dream into reality.

Many people wander through life with big dreams, but they don't have determined thoughts—thoughts that will make them *believe* what it takes, *say* what it takes, and even *change* what it takes to start *doing* what it takes and moving that dream to reality.

Instead, they live in the world of idle thoughts, which may be entertaining, sure, but that's about as far as the thoughts ever go. Dreaming is good. It's a God-given gift to be able to imagine and to dream. Doing is better, because doing—actually acting on your dreams—is what moves your life forward and brings greater fulfillment.

It all starts with thoughts.

In this book, I hope to inspire you through biblical passages and stories, and my own personal experiences, to stop thinking idly and start thinking with intent and determination—to start building "mental maps" that will get you moving in the right direction. Maps that will lead you to the good life and the good destiny that God has in store for you.

YOU DETERMINE WHERE YOU GO IN LIFE

Destiny isn't fate. It's not firm. It's not something that just *happens* to you or something that is going to happen no matter what.

No. *You* are the architect of your own life. *You* have free will. You have choices that you can make that will determine your future, and that puts you in the driver's seat. You may not have picked the car! You may not have picked the town you're in! But, you still have power because you still have free will and choice.

Sure, there are events that happen which might put you in the right place at the right time . . . but if you don't choose to *do* the right thing, in that moment, nothing is going to happen!

It's sort of like health and money. It doesn't matter how healthy you are. If you don't have any money, you ain't going anywhere! And, you can have all the money in the world, but if you're as sick as a dog, you ain't going anywhere either!

A God-given destiny is sort of like that. Certain things have to be in line for you to get the best result, but ultimately, *you* are going to determine where you go and what you do in this life.

Nobody is a puppet. God created this earth and the Bible says that He gave it to the children of men (Psalm 115:16), which is you and me. We have to take ownership over what is ours, or we will lose it. Our choices in this life make a difference, but nothing happens without thoughts, which is what mental mapping is all about.

What will we allow ourselves to believe that we can accomplish? What will we do with the good thoughts, good ideas, and good concepts that God has given us? Are these thoughts good? Are they worth pursuing? Do they make us feel passionate? Are they God's way of nudging us to fulfill His good plan, which is His will for our lives?

Can we take those good thoughts and build upon them day by day and reach the good life God has for us? Yes, we can. Abraham did it. Thousands of Christians do it every day, and even nonbelievers can use the principle and see some results.

Taking a thought that you believe is God-revealed and praying about it, focusing on it, and letting it develop into an idea, which produces an action, which leads to more actions on the path to God's good plan for your life . . . well, that's mental mapping, and anybody can do it and see results.

MENTAL MAPPING IS A SPIRITUAL CONCEPT

Mental mapping is a spiritual concept, and spiritual concepts always apply to our lives in a real way, even if they don't appear to do so on the surface.

The Bible tells us that spiritual things, such as mental mapping, are foolish to those who only think naturally.

> But the natural man receiveth not the things of the Spirit of God: for they are foolishness unto him: neither can he know them, because they are spiritually discerned.
> But he that is spiritual judgeth all things, yet he himself is judged of no man.
> For who hath known the mind of the Lord, that he may instruct Him? But we have the mind of Christ.
> 1 CORINTHIANS 2:14–16

So, our spirit can embrace our intellect, but our intellect cannot embrace our spirit. It takes the "mind of Christ" to think beyond the natural.

When Christ comes to live within our heart, we gain the ability to start *thinking* higher, to break free from our old habits, and start thinking new thoughts—higher thoughts.

That verse above says that we have "the mind of Christ" . . . so, what's He thinking? Does it match up with your thoughts? "Christ" means *anointed*. It's a divine style of thinking that isn't bound to just regular old thoughts.

The mind of Christ is a mind full of faith. This may seem totally crazy in the "natural" way of thinking, but is in fact the way God works. Jesus Christ was a visionary in every way, including the way He thought, and He has a totally different visionary-style thinking that we can adopt and start to use today, right here and right now.

Let me warn you. When you start using the mind of Christ, people will think you're crazy. So what! They think I'm crazy! I don't care! If you want to do anything great for God or for this world, or even just for your family, you must get to the point where you don't care what other people think . . . you're going to do the right thing and follow your mental map anyway!

Remember, you're not living for people, you're living for God. If you have a big dream, you will have to think beyond natural thinking. Just figure that most of the people in history who have done phenomenal things were called crazy because others couldn't see what they saw. People will always attack what they don't understand.

Sometimes, though, the one you're going to have to fight the most is *you!*

DON'T FOCUS ON YOUR SHORTCOMINGS

Man, all those years ago, when God first dropped the idea of sharing the Gospel on worldwide television in my mind, I could have backed away from those thoughts and stayed right where I was. I could have let the thoughts about my shortcomings stay in my mind, because, believe me, they came in like a flood!

You see, your natural mind will work against you, if you let it. So you have to make a decision to fight off "natural thoughts" and think higher, which is God's way—with the mind of Christ.

When God told me I would be on worldwide television preaching His Gospel, I could have said, "Oh, that's for somebody else to do, not me."

I could have looked at my stature—I'm short.

I could have listened to my voice—I'm Cajun.

I could have looked at my background—I'm an ex-rocker who had a problem with booze, women, and drugs. Look, I drank enough whisky to float a few boats. I took trips and never left my house! My generation is the late 1960s and 1970s. I'm talking Led Zeppelin, Grand Funk, early ZZ Top days. I had chocolate-brown hair down the middle of my back and boozy breath that could have knocked down a house. Nobody was looking at me and thinking, *Hey, that's a future preacher.* No, they were looking at me thinking, *That's a boy headed for cirrhosis of the liver!*

If you knew me back then, you would have never in a million years thought that I'd accept Jesus as my Savior and one day be preaching His Gospel or talking about mental mapping . . . and I wouldn't have, either. But here I am! We'll get to that later on!

FROM THINKING TO SAYING

You see, once I became a minister and God gave me that thought about sharing His Word in a mass-media way, I made a quality decision to let the seedling of that God-given idea resonate in my mind. I knew what God had done for me and I knew that, if He could help me, He could help anyone.

The more I thought about worldwide television, the more I digested it as a possibility. The more I allowed that thought to stay, the more it became a part of my own vision for my future work for the Lord. I began to "see" myself doing it, in my own mind—not to bring glory to myself, by no means, but to see others hearing the Gospel and coming into a new life with Christ, just as I had done. I was mental mapping and I didn't even know it.

Pretty soon the thought of sharing His Word on such a large scale became so real to me that I *knew* it would come to pass . . . even though, looking at my life at the time, it was as far away as the moon.

Then I made a step beyond thoughts. I started talking about it. To use a scripture, I started to *"calleth those things which be not as though they were"* (Romans 4:17).

So, not only did I picture what I believed was my destiny in my own mind, but I also began to speak out the dream with my mouth. It became part of my prayer life to touch more people for God. I quoted scripture to myself every day about Christ's command to *"Go ye into all the world and preach the Gospel to every creature"* (Mark 16:15). Even though I was chock-a-block full of shortcomings, I refused to speak little of myself. I chose to look ahead and speak about my future, as Romans 4:17 says, and decided to begin pushing myself toward my destiny.

Was I doing anything about it in the natural world? Not yet. I was still working in the area of thoughts and words. To put it in biblical terms, I was living by my faith and by what I could *not* see . . . because nothing was happening that I could see in the natural world. It was all still inside of me.

SPIRITUAL RESISTANCE

Now, unlike many things that God had told me to do in the past, when I got determined in my thoughts, I didn't get a lick of spiritual resistance about my future television ministry. In the past, whatever good thing I wanted to accomplish usually came with some kind of fight. It seemed like something would always jump up to try to steal away what I was praying and goaling for. But with this, there was none of that mess!

At first I couldn't figure out why nothing bad was happening. It was a huge vision for me and I wondered, *Why isn't the devil fighting me on this? Why am I not having problems?*

You see, I know a lot of people don't believe in the devil . . . but that doesn't change the fact that darkness most certainly exists in this world. That's a basic tenet of the Christian faith and one I'm not backing off of. There is a devil. The spiritual world is real. End of statement. Whether somebody believes it or not doesn't change anything. Think of it this way: I can choose not to believe that Paris really exists, but people are going to be eating baguettes there tomorrow nevertheless.

Ephesians 6:12 says it best when it says: *"For we wrestle not against flesh and blood, but against principalities, against powers, against the rulers of the darkness of this world, against spiritual wickedness in high places."* In other words, problems don't come from *people*. We don't wrestle or fight with *people*. We fight with principalities, powers, and the rulers of darkness in this world—we fight against what is dark in the world. I like to say that principalities can work through person-alities! Not that somebody giving me trouble is full of the devil, but am I saying that some people are motivated by dark thoughts, dark deeds, or dark whatever? Yeah! I am! Because that's a fact of life.

Now, I know how life works when it comes to ideas the Lord has given me. Problems usually are thrown at me, but I know that the purpose of the conflict is just to steer me off my course, to break me down, and make me give up. I also know that if I press through, believe God, and don't buckle to the pressure, I'm going to outlast the problems. That's the way it always is for me.

Well, I thought about TV, and then it hit me—and it was pretty simple . . . the devil didn't fight me because he didn't believe it would ever happen!

You see, my goal was in the realm of the "unseen" and, as a flesh-devil, he couldn't fathom that a Cajun boy like me, who didn't have eloquent speech or the finances to make it across town, could be used by God in such a big way.

What's the key here? He didn't *see* how it could ever happen—sight, one of the five senses.

GOD'S IDEA, GOD'S WAYS, MY MANIFESTATION

Well, my faith progressed. I started making natural strides toward the goal. Because I was beginning to talk about going on worldwide tele-vision, people around me began to listen. Some scoffed. Some didn't. When I preached at different churches around southeast Louisiana, I shared what God had told me. Pretty soon, I found people wanting to help me with the vision.

Now, many times, I wouldn't even mention what God had told me. I'd just preach my message. After the services, I had people that would just come right up to me and tell me things like, "I really enjoyed the message. You know, you ought to be on TV." Or they'd say, "You have a television personality. You should go on. I think people would like you." If I heard that once, I heard that a hundred times. I knew God was confirming what He'd told me and He was using other people to encourage me. I'd respond to them by saying, "Thank you, I appreciate it, but I don't have the finances for that yet, but, I believe I one day will."

God began opening people's eyes to my calling. When I first started preaching, nobody saw that in me. But suddenly, after God dropped that idea in my heart, it was as if a light turned on. I began to say it and others began to see it. Then, without any provocation, people who came to see my services began asking me about being a partner with my ministry. At that time, I did not have a concept of partners—which are regular givers to Christian work. People would just come up to me and say something like, "I want to partner with you and give toward you going on television."

What was happening? God was happening! My mental map started coming out of my mouth. The more I said, "I'm going on television," the more determination I was putting behind the idea and, in turn, the more others began to see it, too.

Now, I didn't have the money and I never once raised money for this goal either. But once people started telling me they wanted to be my partner, I began to accept them as partners in this ministry.

You see, I knew that they didn't just want to see my face on the tube . . . they wanted the same thing I wanted, which was and still is to see people's lives changed by the message of Christ. They wanted people to hear my take on the Gospel because, to them, I was real and plainspoken and even, sometimes, kind of funny!

Well, enough people started to give regularly to my ministry toward a future television ministry that I could move forward practically, too. I began to research my local area and see what options were open to me—which was an action based on a belief that I, along with many others, were united about.

As I got enough finances into my ministry to make the first move, I called Cox Production Company in the city of New Orleans, Louisiana, and found out what it would cost to have them film me preaching straight to the camera. They told me, and I hired them for one week's worth of work to just shoot me preaching to the camera. I went in every day with my Bible and what God had put on my heart to preach on, and in a week I did about twenty-five shows. I hired a company to create an intro and exit to my program. All the while, people were still sending in their partnership toward this idea and I was still preaching at churches, as I still do today.

I bought some time on the local Cox Cable Company and began to air my program. I immediately began to get responses. On my show, I gave my ministry address and phone number, and people began to respond with prayer requests, questions, invitations for me to minister at other churches, requests to purchase messages on tape, and financial partnership, too. God was with me and He led more and more people to watch my program.

Well, one day at my office a fax came in. It was from Trinity Broadcasting Network (TBN), a Christian network seen all over the world. It was a contract. My wife, Cathy, and I thought there was some kind of mistake. We hadn't called TBN.

We read the contract and it offered us one year of free airtime on their worldwide network—FREE. We called to ask if there was some kind of mistake since we hadn't called them and they hadn't called us. They said, "No, no mistake" and told us that they wanted my program. They saw something in me that they thought would help their network and wanted to just give me the time. Now, I shouted! That mental map—those determined thoughts—that had produced faith, ideas, and action had come straight into reality.

Within weeks, I was on worldwide television with TBN, who continued to give me airtime for about five years. During that time, my ministry exploded. I became one of the most popular programs on the network. More people watched, more people's lives were changed, and more praise reports came pouring in of people who were saved and helped by God. More people began attending my meetings and more people became partners toward my goal of world evangelism through television, which in turn helped me to buy time on secular stations like ABC, NBC, etc.

This is how God worked on my behalf. Did I have struggles during that beginning time? No. By the time I signed the contract with the local Cox Cable Company, that idiot devil was so taken off-guard that God could use somebody like me that there was practically no time for him to make trouble. That first deal was done—quick and clean, a transaction as smooth as silk—and before the devil knew it, the thing started snowballing and I was broadcasting the Gospel of the Lord Jesus Christ on worldwide television! My mental map became my reality.

CHAPTER 2

A TOWER OF IMAGINATION

IMAGINATION IS POWERFUL. It's God-given and worth using. In the Bible, there is a story about imagination that I believe is really interesting. It is the story of the Tower of Babel. At the beginning of this story, we find out that everyone on earth spoke the same language. By the end of the story, we have the same people speaking different languages.

Most Christians believe that this was God's way of causing people to move out of that one place and start settling in different places around the earth, but what I want you to notice most about the story is the power of human imagination. Read it with me now.

> *And the whole earth was of one language, and of one speech.*
>
> *And it came to pass, as they journeyed from the east, that they found a plain in the land of Shinar; and they dwelt there.*
>
> *And they said one to another, Go to, let us make brick, and burn them thoroughly. And they had brick for stone, and slime had they for mortar.*

And they said, Go to, let us build us a city and a tower, whose top may reach unto heaven; and let us make us a name, lest we be scattered abroad upon the face of the whole earth.

And the LORD came down to see the city and the tower, which the children of men builded.

And the LORD said, Behold, the people is one, and they have all one language; and this they begin to do: and now nothing will be restrained from them, which they have imagined to do.

Go to, let us go down, and there confound their language, that they may not understand one another's speech.

So the LORD scattered them abroad from thence upon the face of all the earth: and they left off to build the city.

Therefore is the name of it called Babel; because the LORD did there confound the language of all the earth: and from thence did the LORD scatter them abroad upon the face of all the earth.

GENESIS 11:1–9

Were all of these people good or righteous? No, they weren't. Yet, God said that He had to restrain them, because what they imagined to do, they could do! And, obviously He didn't want them doing it!

God's reasons for stopping them are His own, but obviously He didn't want them building something and trying to make a name for themselves when they should be scattering and populating the rest of the earth. God is spiritual, but He's also practical. Babies needed to be made. People needed to move. Things needed to get going!

Now, unlike a lot of traditionalists, I believe that these people didn't actually build one part of that tower. I believe that they *made* bricks and slime for mortar, but I don't believe that they ever actually began building the tower.

I believe that they *imagined* that they'd built the tower—I believe that they made a corporate mental map.

These people dreamed, planned, and mentally mapped out that tower from top to bottom, from beginning to end. And although they were not all righteous, they were all thinking one way, which is powerful. They had faith in themselves to do something that seemed impossible.

They were in agreement. They had one mind and one accord. Their imagination was corporately focused . . . and God took notice. Read the Scripture passage again and you will see that these people were talking to one another and saying, "Let us go and do this or that." That's what I call planning-stage talk.

They never once said that they were stacking bricks. I believe that they didn't say it because they didn't do it! In my opinion, the Tower of Babel was built in the realm of imagination—they saw it in their minds and God saw it there, too! He knew they could do it, but He had other plans!

The point I want to make here is simple. Thoughts are powerful. Imagination is powerful. Focused and determined thoughts become mental maps that are taking you somewhere. Those types of thoughts aren't just dreams, they are pre-actions! They are the passionate thoughts that get you moving and doing. In my opinion, building a mental map was part of the process of the Tower of Babel's construction just as much as forming the bricks.

Did they finish building the tower? Yes, they finished building it in their *minds*. You see, to them, it was already complete before it was ever begun or finished. This is faith, and God notices this kind of thinking because it's His kind of thinking, and it works.

The Bible tells us that this is what God did when He created the universe. He built a mental map. He saw it from beginning to end and all the stages in between. I believe that He even thought, *I am going to create some Louisiana wetlands and put a boy named Jesse on them. He's going to be short. He's going to have white hair and white teeth, but I'm going to bless him with joy!* Yeah, I believe it!

Look, God knows how many hairs we've got on our head, so don't you think He knows *who* we are, *where* we're from, and *how* we're going to look? God loves our diversity!

WHAT IF WE ARE GOING THE WRONG WAY?

It's important to know that God responds to mental mapping. If we are going His way, which takes us on the right path, He will never stop us. But, if we are going against His way, which is against our own good, divine destiny, then God has every sovereign right to either (1) let us go our own way or (2) stop us. It's up to Him to choose if He will or will not intervene.

In the story of the Tower of Babel, we can see that their map got in the way of God's plan to populate the earth. So, He chose to change things by passing out languages. Does this mean that He will always stop you from going the wrong way? No. Remember, all God *has* to do is what He's already *said* He'll do in His Word—nothing more and nothing less.

God has already sent His Son, then the Holy Spirit. He has already given us free will and access to His great love, grace, and mercy. The rest is up to us. *We* choose what we are going to do in this life.

We choose whether we're going to pray and seek Him concerning our destiny or whether we're going to wander aimlessly through life. All of us have been given free will to go toward or against our divine destiny—to become the person we were created to be or not.

Your future is up to you. Build a mental map like these people at the Tower of Babel did, and I promise you, God will take notice of your faith. Like He told them, He'll tell you, "*. . . nothing will be restrained from them, **which they have imagined to do**"* (Genesis 11:6).

There is nothing that you can't do!

GOD HAS A GOOD PLAN FOR YOUR LIFE

Personality and talent alone can't promote a person in life. Psalm 75:6–7 says, "*For promotion cometh neither from the east, nor from the west, nor from the south. But God is the judge: He putteth down one, and setteth up another."* In other words, promotion doesn't really come from the east, west, or the south . . . it comes from the north, the heavens, which is where the Lord resides! Promotion comes from God and from operating according to the principles He set into place in the beginning of time. What you sow, you will reap. What you think about, you will become. What you speak, you will draw into your life. Where is your focus? Where is your faith? Because that is what is going to determine your destiny.

Very few things are as important as faith. Hebrews 11:6 says, *"But without faith it is impossible to please Him: for He that cometh to God must believe that He is, and that He is a rewarder of them that diligently seek Him."*

Do you want the best life you can have? Then it starts with making God a priority. First, you have to believe that He exists. That's baseline faith. Then you have to act on that faith. You must let His spirit, which is within you, and His Word be your guide—and be confident about it.

Can you be successful without God? Yes, to a degree, you can. Without God in your life, you can accomplish a lot, but you will never have true peace or real and lasting success without having that connection with God.

Money is not success. It is a byproduct of success. The truly successful life that God wants for you is one of spiritual blessing, physical blessing, and financial blessing—a life that includes salvation, joy, peace of mind, good relationships, health, financial ease, or even freedom, and more. It's a way of life that you can pass down to future generations.

Without God, you can practice good principles and see one or two facets of success in life, but with Him, your soul finds rest.

You have potential. God didn't make any mistakes when He made you. So, don't sell yourself short. You may not be able to do much on your own or you may be able to do a lot on your own, but either way, it's the God-centered path that is going to make you a true success—and that path is made easier by faith.

THE TIME IS NOW

Faith is a "now" concept. The most famous verse about faith is in Hebrews 11:1. There it says, *"Now faith is the substance of things hoped for, the evidence of things not seen."* I want you to notice the first three words in this verse: *"Now faith is. . . ."* Notice that it doesn't say "Later faith is . . ." No, faith is a "now" concept.

In fact, notice that the very first word in this verse isn't faith at all. It's "Now." Now is the day of salvation. Now is the time to get on track with God's plan for your life. Now is the time to start building mental maps.

Now is a word that connotes time. Why is God interested in time? Because He knows you've only got so much of it! God wants the best for you, and His best starts *now.* Our God is a Creator. He's omnipotent. He's not a "might be" or "you never know" kind of God. He's detailed and purposeful, and He has good plans for your life that can start today. Regardless of whether you're twelve or eighty, God can help you fulfill a good plan for whatever life you have ahead of you.

In Jeremiah 29:11, God says, *"For I know the plans I have for you,' declares the LORD, 'plans to prosper you and not to harm you, plans to give you hope and a future'"* (NIV).

When you put your faith in God, you can be sure that His plans for your life are only good. He wants to prosper you in every way—first spiritually, then physically, financially, and in every other way in life. From your relationships to your peace of mind, God promises that there is no harm in His plan for your life. He only wants to give you a hope and a future, a prosperous and good future.

Anything that comes to harm you is not from God. Harm may come from living in this sin-sick world. Harm may come from being around a person driven by dark thoughts or deeds toward you. Harm may even come because you have self-destructive thoughts or habits . . . but nothing that is harmful comes from God, according to the Bible in Jeremiah 29:11. He is good. Get your mind around that so that you can move forward and stop thinking that it's His will to hurt you, because it isn't.

It is your *faith* in God and in His good plan for your life that has the ability to start creating a good future for you. Your faith will help you to solidify your mental map, to the point that the two will merge into one powerful force that you can move forward with and see results.

WITH GOD, YOU ARE AN OVERCOMER

Will trouble come your way even if you have faith? You better know it! Of course it will. Trouble is part of life, so don't act like it's something foreign and strange when it comes your way. Instead, learn to deal with it so you can keep your peace.

Jesus said, *"These things I have spoken unto you, that in Me ye might have peace. In the world ye shall have tribulation: but be of good cheer; I have overcome the world"* (John 16:33).

Jesus died on the cross so that you could be saved. He died so that you could live—really live—by breaking free from the old path of destruction and starting to walk on the good path of life. Receiving Him as your Savior and Lord is the first step to finding your place in this world.

So, when Jesus commands you to be of good cheer, He is really saying, "Smile, laugh, let your heart be light. When trouble arises, don't let it steal your joy. I overcame all the sin and destruction you see and because I paid the price, you can have peace. You can walk in My victory no matter what is going on around you. You can smile knowing that you will overcome it all!"

People see me smiling all the time and they think that I don't have any problems. That's not true. Many of my smiles have been birthed in persecution. Obstacles arise in my life all the time, but I made a decision a long time ago that God is with me.

God is my refuge, and His joy is what gives me strength—not my joy, but His joy. It's something He gives to me when I refuse to let circumstances sway my faith in Him. I just rest in His peace. I partake of His joy. I know that Jesus has overcome because of His work on the cross. So, I am being of good cheer. No matter what trouble comes to try and rock my foundation, my faith is in God. With God, I am an overcomer and you are, too!

TAKE OFF THE LIMITS

You didn't have a choice how you began in life. You couldn't pick your parents or the situation you grew up in. But the moment you realize that your past doesn't have to dictate your future—that you are a new creature in Christ—you start taking possession of your destiny.

Every time you let go of those old limitations and realize your position in Christ, you are propelling yourself toward your destiny. Every time you ask God to guide your steps and choose to follow His Word, you are giving yourself divine tools for living, tools that will help you to move away from what harms you and toward what is in God's good plan for your life.

When you see your faith in God as a "now" concept, you are saying, "God, I know that You are making a way for me today." You are agreeing that His wisdom and guidance isn't something He *might* give to you today; it's something He *will* give. All you have to do is ask.

Wisdom is part of your inheritance as a child of God, but it is something that must be received from the Lord.

> *If any of you lack wisdom, let him ask of God, that giveth to all men liberally, and upbraideth not; and it shall be given him.*
>
> *But let him ask in faith, nothing wavering. For he that wavereth is like a wave of the sea driven with the wind and tossed.*
>
> *For let not that man think that he shall receive any thing of the Lord.*
>
> *A double minded man is unstable in all his ways.*
>
> *JAMES 1:5–8*

Notice that you need faith to get wisdom. Your prayers can't be spoken in doubt, because God honors faith. He doesn't honor double-mindedness.

When you pray in faith, you step into a powerful way of life. You choose to believe in Someone greater than yourself. Through your prayers and actions, you're implying, *God, not my will be done, but Yours!* You trust in the One that is leading you on the path that you are meant to go.

ALL THINGS ARE POSSIBLE: BELIEVE IT

I once read a quote that said, "The greatest thing in the world is not so much where we stand as in which direction we are moving."

I believe that God wants you to push beyond what you think you can do because with Him, *all* things are possible. He's a limitless God, and He wants you to think on a higher level than what you're thinking now, so that you can get rid of your preconceived ideas of what you can and can't do. Those negative preconceived ideas will kill your ability to reach your destiny.

Start by cleaning up your everyday thought-life. Proverbs 23:7 reveals some real wisdom when it says, *"For as he thinketh in his heart, so is he."*

In other words, you'll become a product of what you think about. I'm not talking about random thoughts. I'm talking about your determined and rooted-down-deep thoughts such as the preconceived ideas you have about yourself—what you can be and what you can do.

Thoughts are like mental maps, and they are taking you somewhere. They can take you into the realm of the seen—what you can do on your own. Or they can take you into the realm of the unseen—the place that requires God's guidance and help, the life that He has for you.

Don't let hesitancy about your own abilities stifle your life. Push out the negative things people have told you about yourself. Remember, you're not going through this life alone. God is with you.

IF YOU CAN'T SEE FAITH, NEITHER CAN THE DEVIL!

Faith is a substance. It's evidence. It's something you can't see. It's a spiritual force. Common sense says you should accept only things that you can *see* as evidence. But to God, when it comes to faith, it's what you *can't* see that is real evidence. *"Now faith is the substance of things hoped for, **the evidence of things not seen**"* (Hebrews 11:1).

Why did God put faith in the realm of the unseen? Because if you can't see it, neither can the devil! A lot of people think that just because the devil is at war with God that he is spiritual. He's not. He lost his spiritual connection the moment he rebelled against God. The devil is a "flesh-devil" in that he works in the realm of the flesh. He is not spiritually minded. He has no faith.

You, on the other hand, *are* spiritual. If you've accepted Christ as your Savior, you have been washed clean of all unrighteousness. Now, when God looks at you, He sees you through the blood of His Son— the atoning sacrifice of Jesus Christ, which makes you righteous in God's sight.

But you still live in this sin-filled world. So, how do you get around the dirt of this world and stay on God's path for your life? By renewing your mind to the Word of God. By letting the heart-change that you made at the point of your salvation become a lifestyle change. You can't do it on your own because you've got years of bad habits behind you—habits that probably don't include having faith in God. But God has made a way for you to change.

In Romans 12:2, it says, *"And be not conformed to this world: but be ye transformed by the renewing of your mind, that ye may prove what is that good, and acceptable, and perfect will of God."* What is the good, acceptable, and perfect will of God for your life? What is it that God created you to do and to be?

This is something that only you and God know. As a believer, you are destined to overcome, and you are challenged to share God's gift with others. It's part of the corporate destiny of the church.

But your personal road in life is between you and God. If you don't know what it is, draw close to Him. Let His Word transform your way of thinking so that you can think beyond what you know right now.

If you conform to this world and the way it thinks, you won't find God's plan for your life. But if you allow God, who loves you and has only good plans for your life, to start changing the way you think about yourself and the world around you, then you are going to make your mark in life! You'll find that you are on the right path and God will show you what to do in life.

God will reveal your divine destiny to you, day by day and situation by situation. As you draw closer to Him, He may even give you a vision of what is to come, but it is all going to start with knowing Him as your Savior and following the great wisdom in His Word.

The more you obey Romans 12:2, the more you are going to see things God's way—through the eyes of faith. Then you're going to start living in the realm of the unseen. This is where I live. I am always using my faith and, consequently, it's always working for me.

You see, **God's plan for your life won't make it into the realm of the *seen* until you birth it in the realm of the *unseen*.** The realm of the unseen is the place of faith, and that is where you are going to start building your mental map on the road to your divine destiny.

If you have a dream, follow it. Focus your mind on it every day. Cultivate that dream in your heart. Don't let it slip away.

Put your vision or dream in the powerful realm of the unseen. Forget about "can't" and "never will." That's a bunch of junk. Take off the limits in your mind first. Accept the dream, idea, or vision God put in you. Then start using that creative substance within you called faith to build a better life for yourself, your family, and the world around you.

CHAPTER 3

ABRAHAM, THE FATHER OF MENTAL MAPPING

FAITH IS A funny thing. It'll take you to places you never thought you'd go. One of the greatest men of faith was Abraham. Many call him the father of faith; I like to call him the father of mental mapping.

Faith sent Abraham out to walk in a desert, without knowing where he was going—and the man was seventy-five years old! He probably was missing a few teeth, and his family probably thought he was missing a few brain cells, too.

Yet, according to Hebrews chapter 11, Abraham *". . . went out, not knowing whither he went."* His purpose? To follow after God and step into his divine destiny.

> By faith Abraham, when he was called to go out into
> a place which he should after receive for an inheritance,
> obeyed; and he went out, not knowing whither he went.
>
> By faith he sojourned in the land of promise, as in a
> strange country, dwelling in tabernacles with Isaac and
> Jacob, the heirs with him of the same promise:

For he looked for a city which hath foundations, whose builder and maker is God.

HEBREWS 11:8–10

Was Abraham really looking for a city that was physically built, brick by brick, by God? No, he was looking for a place with a spiritual foundation. But Abraham didn't just leave because he thought it was a good idea. This old man heard the voice of God! He'd gone to Egypt, inherited Canaan, and dealt with his problems of bringing his nephew, Lot, already. Now, he was walking smack-dab in the middle of the road that led to his divine destiny.

You see, Abraham had built a mental map and he was getting after it! He had a vision in which God had not only spoken to him, but had also given him a mental picture of the future.

After these things the word of the LORD came unto Abram in a vision, saying, Fear not, Abram: I am thy shield, and thy exceeding great reward.

And Abram said, Lord GOD, what wilt thou give me, seeing I go childless, and the steward of my house is this Eliezer of Damascus?

And Abram said, Behold, to me Thou hast given no seed: and, lo, one born in my house is mine heir.

And, behold, the word of the LORD came unto him, saying, This shall not be thine heir; but he that shall come forth out of thine own bowels shall be thine heir.

And He brought him forth abroad, and said, Look now toward heaven, and tell the stars, if thou be able to number them: and He said unto him, So shall thy seed be.

GENESIS 15:1–5

God believes in the power of imagination. He wants you to visualize your future, to use it as a jumping-off point in your faith. I want you to notice that God didn't just *tell* Abraham that he would have an heir through his own body; He brought him out and *showed* him what his seed would one day look like—like the stars that filled the sky.

What did God give Abraham? A mental map to take him on the road to his divine destiny. You can take this as a lesson on the importance of seeing your future with the eyes of faith. Now, it was Abraham's decision to believe. He could have dismissed it all and gone back to his old life. He could have used the excuse, "But I'm old! I'm at the end of my life!" He didn't, and that's why we call him the father of faith today. *"And he believed in the LORD; and He counted it to him for righteousness"* (Genesis 15:6).

Beware of the deadening influence of routine and its twin brother, the enslaving power of custom. Abraham was an old man, but he didn't let his routines and customs get in the way of his destiny.

Abraham became the father of faith, the father of mental mapping.

YOU CAN'T HAVE WHAT YOU SPEAK AGAINST

Was it easy for Abraham to fulfill his destiny? No, not only was he old, but his wife was barren. She couldn't have children as a young woman, and now she was past her prime, so to speak. So, Abraham was right in the middle of a situation that would cause most people to simply give up.

Sounds like God, doesn't it? He never asks you for how much you have in the bank when He tells you what He wants to do in your life. He doesn't look at where you are. He looks at where you're going. Besides, God knows that He's with you and that, with Him on your side, you can do anything.

When God gives you a vision, it's almost always going to be bigger than what you can do on your own. That's His way of doing things. You just have to accept it! Let this word from Jesus sink into your heart: *"With men this is impossible; but with God all things are possible"* (Matthew 19:26). See your vision in your mind and accept it knowing that, with God, ALL things are possible!

Next, your mouth has to get involved. Don't fall into the trap of speaking against your destiny. Don't talk negatively about your dreams because, whatever you speak against, you'll never get.

If you speak against prosperity, you won't have to worry about being prosperous. You'll live broke all the days of your life! If you speak against healing, you can take it to the bank that you will never be healed. You're going to be sick! And, if you speak against salvation, guess what? You won't be saved either . . . the devil will be waiting with a grin when you step across the heated floor of Hell.

You can't receive what you speak against. That's an important point. So, watch your lips! It's part of having faith.

You must look beyond what you can see, even if your senses give you no assurance. Making it to your destiny depends on it.

ANXIETY PROPELS DISOBEDIENCE

Where was Abraham's wife in all of this? She had to have even greater faith because God didn't take her out and show her the stars, even though her destiny was to conceive and give birth to a miracle baby. Instead, she had to have faith in both God and Abraham.

As time went on, Sarah became filled with anxiety about her situation. She wanted a baby so bad that she began to think outside of the vision. She began to doubt God's promise and to take matters into her own hands. Her anxiety propelled her to contemplate disobedience.

Sarah looked around the camp and saw her servant, Hagar. She thought about it and eventually came to see that young woman as her only hope. It was rational to her natural mind, but totally against the promise. She didn't care. She asked Abraham to sleep with Hagar so that they could have a baby—bad idea!

Hagar was the first surrogate mother that the Bible speaks of, except Hagar really didn't have a choice in the matter. So, it was a wrong situation all around.

Now, what I want you to see is that Abraham didn't fight Sarah much! He thought, *Okay, Mama, whatever you want. Come here, Hagar!* Instead of standing up for righteousness and reminding his wife of what God had said, Abraham gave in. He slept with the woman, got her pregnant, and it wasn't long before family problems started taking over. Let's face it, two women having a stake in the life of one man is never a good idea! Jealousy is bound to happen, and in this case, it did!

JEWS AND ARABS—FAMILY PROBLEMS!

Abraham was eighty-six when his son, Ishmael, was born—and it wasn't easy for Hagar or Sarah. There was hurt, anger, and resentment between the two women and the tension got so thick that, eventually, it split up the family. Abraham was torn up about it. It hurt him to see his family split into two.

The truth is that Abraham's family is still split up today. The Jewish line courses through Abraham and *Sarah* (who's promised child we'll get to in a second). But it is through Abraham and *Hagar*, who was an Egyptian, that we get the Arab people of our world. Today, they are predominantly Muslim. So, when we talk about the Jews and the Palestinians, we're talking about ancient brothers—one group who stuck to the original Jewish faith and the other who chose to follow Muhammad's teachings.

The Word says that this heir would be, "'. . . *a wild man; his hand will be against every man, and every man's hand will be against him; and he shall dwell in the presence of all his brethren'*" (Genesis 16:12). Does that sound like the Middle East to you? It's called family problems! They are still happening today.

Some people read that scripture and think that God was condemning Ishmael and his descendents. It's not true. God didn't *make* Ishmael a contentious man. God was simply looking into the future and seeing what *Satan* would do to bring anger, strife, and division into the family, from the very beginning until now.

You see, this is what people do not understand—the war on terrorism isn't just a physical war . . . it's a *spiritual* war.

So, who is the real enemy? Simple. It's the one filled with the most hate—and I believe that is the devil, who has tricked a great many good people into believing his lies. The radical Muslim has a problem with hate.

HATE KILLS, STEALS, AND DESTROYS

Hate steals good thoughts. Hate destroys hope and peace. Hate can twist a man's mind to such a degree that he loses the ability to be reasonable . . . even if he started out honestly wanting to do the right thing and make the world he lives in a better place.

Hate can turn a good man into a rabid, foaming-at-the-mouth killer. You can't pin that kind of thing on God . . . but you can pin it on religion.

What a man believes will affect how he thinks. What a man thinks will affect what he does. So, if a man is passionate about hating, then you can take it to the bank that some conflict is coming! He's got a fuse hanging out his window and he's waiting for somebody, anybody, to come along and strike a match!

The mind of a radical Muslim is hard to understand. The terrorists truly believe that it is noble to strap bombs to their children in order to kill somebody they hate. That mind believes it's worth the cost. They think we aren't living right and deserve death. A man can't get to that level of hatred without being conditioned . . . and he can't be conditioned to hate that much unless he's been deceived. And who do you think is the biggest deceiver of all time? You know who *I* think it is!

Jesus said that "the thief" is one who comes "to steal, and to kill, and to destroy" in John 10:10. Is hate a thief? Does it kill? Does it steal? Does it destroy? You better know it does! Turn on your TV and watch the news, buddy—hate is killing somebody *every* day.

As human beings who value life, it is important for us to recognize the *source* of hatred so that we can fight it from the right standpoint—a spiritual standpoint.

HATE DOESN'T JUST "HAPPEN"

Hate is grown. It starts in the mind. If a man lets hate stick around, it will eventually deepen, drop into his heart, and become ingrained. Eventually he'll reach the point of hard-heartedness and may even find himself teaching his children to hate . . . and thinking that it's a good thing to do. That's exactly what has happened throughout the radical Muslim community. Do I hate the radical Muslims? No! I don't hate anybody! I'm a Christian, so I believe that God has grace and mercy for everyone, no matter what they've done. I honestly think a man can change, no matter who he is or what he's been taught. Even the worst-acting man in the world can stop living the way that he's been living. If a man has a true change of heart, he can change the way he thinks and lives his life—that change can mean the difference between passing hate to his children or not.

The Apostle Paul was a highly educated man but a true persecutor of Christians. He killed them and thought it was the right thing to do. But then he had an experience with God that changed his heart. It led him onto a different road in life and eventually he became a disciple of Christ. Paul wrote two-thirds of the New Testament . . . and he started out as a killer. *That's* what God can do to change a man's heart. God recognized the value of Paul's passion and turned him from a path of hate and destruction to a path of mercy, grace, goodness, and love. Nobody is hopeless.

It's like this. No matter what kind of hatred you were raised with, if you find out that one day that hatred is killing, stealing, and destroying your life, then you have a God-given right to use your personal authority and make a change. It starts in the heart, but it's a conscious decision of the mind to stop and change direction.

Take me, for instance. I was raised around a lot of prejudiced people. That was just a fact of life growing up in southern Louisiana in the 1950s and 1960s. Yet it bothered me to see prejudice in action from the time I was a very small boy. So, I made a conscious decision *not* to be that kind of man. I spent many afternoons down the street at my old black neighbor's house playing the guitar. I refused to enter into conversations that promoted more racism, and I made a conscious decision to take up for people that I saw were being persecuted because of their race. Later, when I married and had a child, I chose to tell my kid to never judge a man by the color of his skin. I could have gone the way of my parents' generation, but I decided not to.

Today, I preach the goodness, righteousness, and love of God on worldwide television—that includes many parts of the Middle East. I don't do it because I want to convert people. I couldn't convert somebody if I wanted to. Only God can change the heart of a man—I can't "save" anyone.

But I honestly believe every person deserves the right to hear about the love of God and the mercy of God. I did, and it changed my life. I believe that kind of change can happen to anybody. When a man finds the real love of God for himself, he's going to have a hard time strapping bombs to the backs of his children and murdering his brothers . . . even if he once thought it was the right thing to do. God's love and mercy changes the heart.

Okay, I'm nearly done with my commentary on the root issues of the Middle East! One last thing and we'll move on . . . I honestly believe that *both* the Jews and the Arabs can give us great understanding because, after all, they come from the same great father—Abraham.

Abraham had *vision!* Abraham had *faith!* Abraham was even a man of *peace.* Was he perfect? No! Then again, who is? But, God had a plan for his life . . . He has a plan for your life, too.

It gives me real hope to know that when Abraham died, *both* of his sons stood side by side at his funeral . . . they came together because they recognized what *united* them more than what *separated* them. Let's pray they choose to do that again in our lifetime!

All right, now, let's get back to the beginnings of Abraham and Sarah! Their dream will show you that *anything* is possible!

ABRAHAM AND SARAH: DELAYED BUT NOT DISMISSED!

When Abraham and Sarah went outside God's plan, He didn't pitch their destiny out the window. God saw Abraham's original faith and knew that he was swayed by his wife. It didn't stop God's plan, but it did *delay* it and cause many hurts. What could have been a peaceful path turned into more drama than you can shake a stick at!

It wasn't until thirteen years later that God spoke to Abraham about his destiny. And when He did, the Word records that God immediately told Abraham to walk more uprightly. Then, He shared his destiny again.

> *And when Abram was ninety years old and nine, the LORD appeared to Abram, and said unto him, I am the Almighty God; walk before Me, and be thou perfect.*
>
> *And I will make My covenant between Me and thee, and will multiply thee exceedingly.*
>
> *And Abram fell on his face: and God talked with him, saying,*
>
> *As for Me, behold, My covenant is with thee, and thou shalt be a father of many nations.*
>
> *Neither shall thy name any more be called Abram, but thy name shall be Abraham; for a father of many nations have I made thee.*
>
> *And I will make thee exceeding fruitful, and I will make nations of thee, and kings shall come out of thee.*
>
> *And I will establish my covenant between Me and thee and thy seed after thee in their generations for an everlasting covenant, to be a God unto thee, and to thy seed after thee.*
>
> GENESIS 17:1–7

LAUGHTER IS BORN

> *And God said unto Abraham, As for Sarai thy wife, thou shalt not call her name Sarai, but Sarah shall her name be.*
>
> *And I will bless her, and give thee a son also of her:*

yea, I will bless her, and she shall be a mother of nations; kings of people shall be of her.

Then Abraham fell upon his face, and laughed, and said in his heart, Shall a child be born unto him that is an hundred years old? and shall Sarah, that is ninety years old, bear?

GENESIS 17:15–17

Abraham laughed—not in lack of faith, but in sheer astonishment. I bet he was thinking, *Have you seen old Sarah lately? God, we're getting old!* Yet God didn't care about Sarah's age. He wanted Abraham to be the father of many nations, and He wanted Sarah to be the mother of many nations. God had a plan for this woman's life and it included a baby! God loves babies and He was *making* barren women fertile long before doctors starting making the big bucks "practicing" it.

It was never God's plan to establish his covenant between Abraham and Hagar. It was God's plan for Abraham to be faithful to his wife, Sarah, and to encourage her when she was despondent about not yet being pregnant—not give in to her.

Well, after Abraham heard from God again in Genesis 17:15–17, it wasn't long before three men showed up at Abraham's door and said, "*. . . Sarah your wife shall have a son*" (Genesis 18:10, NKJV). It was a prophecy that the men told to Abraham, but Sarah was listening through the tent walls and overheard.

What did Sarah do? She laughed, just like Abraham did when he heard the word from God. But, she wasn't laughing a year later . . . by Genesis 21 Isaac was born, just one year to the time that Abraham heard from God.

Sarah, who was overwhelmed by the humor of bearing and nursing a child at ninety-nine years old said, "*. . . God has made me laugh, so that all who hear will laugh with me*" (Genesis 21:6).

I like to tell elderly people that if their kids are trying to put them in an old folks' home, they should have a baby and freak them all out!

Sound impossible? It is. But, then, with God all things are possible. What He says comes to pass. All He really needed was the faith of the one He told the promise to—Abraham. Sarah just had to agree with Abraham's faith. He obviously had enough for the both of them.

You see, when the dream is told to you . . . you are the one who has got to believe more than anybody else. You can't depend on somebody else. You have to have faith for yourself.

When everybody thought Abraham and Sarah couldn't and wouldn't have a child, God revealed Himself as El Shaddiah. These two couldn't make their parts work. Viagra had not yet been invented. It just wasn't going to happen.

But God came upon the scene. He touched them and Abraham got happy! He probably thought, *Come here, girl!* Sarah, whose womb suddenly opened, obviously had the feeling too! She probably thought, *Get down with your bad self, Abe!* Nine months later, Isaac— laughter—was born!

Your dream, your vision—it may be so impossible that you want to start taking matters into your own hands like Sarah did and figure out a way to "make" it happen, even if it means doing what you know is wrong. That's worry. That's anxiety. Don't let anxiety steal your faith in God's power to make dreams happen. Stick it out.

Have faith in God. Remember your mental map. Do what you know is right. Sure, God can turn any situation around and help you move past mistakes if you make them, but it's better to stay on course. It's better to keep the faith and live in peace!

What you are astonished by, the dream that makes you laugh, *can* happen. So, let the joy of the Lord fill your heart. Let yourself laugh. Don't laugh in doubt, laugh in astonishment. Laugh at your enemy, even if that enemy seems to be time.

Remember, you are going to outlast what you think is in your way. You are going to overcome. God is going to bring you to where you need to be as you trust in Him—He's going to lead you to your divine destiny!

CHAPTER 4

ARE YOUR MEMORIES BIGGER THAN YOUR DREAMS?

EVERY GREAT INVENTION you see began with a dream. The car you drive has its roots in Henry Ford's dream of the automobile. The light that turns on when you hit the switch was conceived in the mind of Thomas Edison.

Mr. Ford was tired of riding horses and set his sights on creating an "automobile," which he called the "Model T." You could get it any color you wanted as long as it was black.

Mr. Edison was tired of lighting his house with gas. The carbon monoxide was giving him headaches. But he didn't invent aspirin to cover up the problem. He began dreaming of a solution to gas. He began thinking about inventing something to give us artificial light. Look at your ceiling right now. Do you see a light bulb? Thank Edison! He invented it!

Even the paper that this book is printed on also has its roots in someone's dream. Praise God we don't have to chip away at a stone tablet! Praise God somebody looked at wood and thought, *Hmm, I bet I could write on that!*

Some of the simplest inventions have been the most life-changing. When I go to the throne, and I'm not talking about Heaven, I praise God for the guy that invented the soft stuff! I'm so glad some guy thought beyond the leaf!

In fact, look around you right now and see the "things" people have invented, built, or made better. Almost every one of them started with a dream, and then developed into a determined thought—a mental map—that became the critical factor in putting action behind the thoughts and getting the job done!

THE PAST NEVER SEES THE FUTURE

Good or bad, it's time to put the past behind you. The past never sees the future. If you feel stifled because you don't have any dreams or goals in life, you're probably living on memories of what you've done in the past. That's no good.

Don't give up on life. There is still more for you to do and see. Are you still breathing? Then you still have the potential to dream. You can still get determined in your thoughts. You can still get ideas, and you can still act on those ideas and accomplish something in your life.

I don't care how old you are. You can be a visionary and you can act on the ideas and dreams God has put on your heart. Think about Abraham. God didn't care that he was an old man when He gave him an idea of his future as the father of many generations.

God doesn't care if you're five years old or ninety-five years old. He sees your potential and the impact you can have on the future, regardless of at what age you're starting. People may want to put you out to pasture, but God never does that. He is with you no matter what. So, don't waste your precious life only dreaming, but not mental mapping. Get determined to be a visionary in your own life—to move forward, to keep on living and learning and doing something. Your destiny doesn't ever end. No, one day, you'll just move from this life to the next, and then your life will just keep on going.

I like to say that if death were punctuation, it would be a comma . . . not a period. Death is not the end. It's a pause before you begin again. The real you is the combination of your spirit and your soul. Your spirit is what becomes re-created or renewed when you accept Christ and your soul is your mind, will, and emotions.

The Bible calls this life a "vapor" in that it goes very quickly. But the reality is that you are going to pass from this life into the next one day. You're going to look back at this life and review all you've done with the One that made you. Nobody is going to be there to judge you but God. So, you might as well do what you feel in your heart to do now, while you're on the earth, and live without regret.

That doesn't mean doing every sinful thing because you think you're never going to have the chance once you pass! No, it means do what is good and right; what you know God has put on your heart to accomplish for yourself and others.

As a Christian, your destiny will include winning the lost to Christ and supporting the work of evangelism around the world. That's just a fact of being a believer. But it will also include using your faith to draw on the power of God for your relationships, your financial prosperity, and your personal health. God cares about it all!

THE CORPORATE DESTINY OF THE CHURCH

Many Christians read books about the revivals of old. They read about the great healing revivals and focus on the past so much that they don't pray about the next revival, the next phase in God's plan for His people. God wants to do a new thing for this generation. It may be similar to the last, in that its focus will be on God, but it won't be exactly the same because God will be dealing with different people with different gifts.

I thank God for the 1947 and 1958 healing revivals with young Oral Roberts, Gordon Lindsay, Jack Coe, and William Brannon. I'm glad they happened. I'm blessed to read books that made accounts of the many revivals God has given us throughout the ages, but I'm not content to live in the past. The past never sees the future. Today is a new day and tomorrow is coming.

As the church, it's our corporate destiny to reach our generation with the Good News. I'm a minister today because I recognize the call of God on my life to be a mouthpiece for Christ. But I'm not at this alone. I'm part of a great big body of believers, all reaching toward the same spiritual goal.

THE POOREST PERSON IS ONE WITHOUT A DREAM

I've heard it said that **the poorest person in the world is not the one without a nickel; it's the one without a dream.** Visionaries dream, and dreams are always the starting point of creating mental maps. You can't get determined about a dream unless you first have one. If you're out of practice, start using your imagination more. Start asking questions. Start by thinking about how you can make things better in whatever area of life you are in.

I am constantly dreaming, constantly believing God will help me reach more people for Him. I imagine all the things that must happen to make my dream a reality. I know what I dream of will come to pass if I have faith in God, in myself, and in the dream.

It's my responsibility to not only dream and be determined in my dream, but also to move in the direction of my dream. I know that if I spend too much of my energy focusing on what other people have done in the past, then I'm living in the past—and again, the past never sees the future. Don't lose your passion for today by living in yesterday. If you dwell too much on what they did, you'll lose focus on what you're going to do.

Focus—you've got to have it to get anything done. Being a visionary takes focus. Look beyond what others have done. Look beyond what you're doing now, too. If you miss this, I promise, you're going to lose out.

The Apostle Paul put it this way. He said, *"Brethren, I count not myself to have apprehended: but this **one thing I do, forgetting those*** *things which are behind, and reaching forth unto those things which are before, I press toward the mark* for the prize of the high calling of God in Christ Jesus" (Philippians 3:13–14).

Paul deliberately dismissed what was behind him and pressed forward in his "mark" or goal toward the prize that was in front of him, which was the high calling of Jesus Christ. This is my mark, too, because I'm a preacher of the Gospel.

Your mark may be in another area of life. It doesn't matter. This is a principle that you can use in whatever sector of life you're in. Forget about the past, focus on your future, and keep pressing on.

ELIMINATE YOUR CONFUSION

Confusion comes when you let too many things muddy up your dreams or ideas. Eliminate the confusion by focusing on your priorities.

Faith in God is a priority. Prayer is a priority. Reminding yourself that God gave you that idea or dream that's in your heart is a priority. The flip side? Wondering how in the world it's ever going to get done is *not* a priority—it's confusion. Listening to people who tell you that you "can't" or "never will" is *not* a priority—it's confusion.

Here's a tip. When you're confused, stop for a moment and just praise God. Thank Him for the dream and lift Him up in praise. Then, pray for clarity and wisdom. Distill your thoughts. If it is anxiety getting in your way, cast all your care upon Christ (1 Peter 5:7).

Don't let negative thoughts ramble on and on. Push them out of your mind. Make a concentrated effort to roll the care of those problems onto the Lord. Remember, confusion breeds confusion. **If you focus on your priorities, you'll eliminate your confusion.**

Mentally, work your way to the bottom line and take things from there. You may not know exactly what to do at first, but God can give you peace knowing that He is going to lead you in the right direction for your life. Learn to lean on the power of praise and prayer, and trust Him—that has to become a habit. And how do you form a new habit? By doing the same thing over and over.

Focusing is a habit for me. Speaking positively is a habit for me. Choosing to believe what God says, instead of what man says, is a habit for me. I can say from experience that, if you make these things a habit for yourself, you're going to get further along in your dream because you won't be wasting time wading in a pool of confusion.

Remember, God sent Abraham on a quest to *"Look for a city which hath foundations whose builder and maker is God"* because He wanted Abraham to walk by faith and fulfill his divine destiny as the father of many nations. God has a plan for your life, too. And to reach it, you've got to take a systematic approach of focusing on your priorities and casting down thoughts that breed confusion.

IT'S THE PERSON WHO HAS NEVER DONE ANYTHING WHO IS SURE NOTHING CAN BE DONE

When you start moving forward, people around you are going to assess where they are in life, and jealousy may rear its ugly head. They may not want to see you stand out or do anything great. They may want you to just stay "with the crowd," so to speak, and not be different.

Accept the fact that there will always be someone in your life who doesn't believe that you can reach your dream, or people may not want you to reach your dream, for whatever reason. Just realize that it's a fact of life for a visionary, so don't get discouraged by them.

The more you walk by faith, the more you'll hear from the doubters. Doubt and faith are at opposite ends of the mental map spectrum—the greater you grow in faith, the more obvious it is to the doubters. They'll think it's their responsibility to pick out all your flaws and cut you down to size—their size, the size of a doubter! Don't take what they say to heart.

Remember that it's the person who has never done anything who is sure nothing can be done.

The truth is that people who tell you that "you can't" aren't really talking to you at all—they're talking to themselves. *They* can't. *They* won't. *They* never will. They want to project their self-doubt onto you. Don't let them. Realize that faith catapults you into another realm of thinking. You are different and capable because you have faith in God. Faith in the God of Creation is what turns "can't," "won't," and "never will" into "can," "will," and "will again!"

It's a crying shame, but it's human nature to tear down the dreams of others. It's a form of competitiveness, but God's nature is to love and encourage others in their dreams. His nature is a "you can do it, I believe in you" type of love, a divine parental love that works in cooperation, not in competition.

When I hear the words, "Jesse, that's impossible!" I know that I'm talking to somebody who doesn't believe in my dream. They don't have any faith in me, so why should I share my precious dream with them?

I don't take anything the naysayers say about my dream to heart. They didn't hear the voice of God. They're just using their rational mind to assess my situation, but **dreams don't get done without somebody thinking beyond the "norm."**

For Edison, it took thinking beyond gaslight to get to his dream of electric light. I bet somebody told him it was a crazy idea. Thank God he didn't listen. For Henry Ford, it took thinking beyond a horse to get to his dream of the automobile. I'm sure he heard that it was "impossible" too, but he kept pressing on. That's how things get done, small or great.

DON'T CAST YOUR PEARLS BEFORE SWINE

You know, everything I've ever believed for I couldn't do. I'll never forget when I first began my ministry. I was driving an old, beat-up Toyota to a meeting and I saw a jet fly overhead and the Lord spoke to my heart, *I'm gonna give you a jet.* I thought, *You've got to be kidding! Whoa, glory!*

At that moment, I was on my way to preach at a church in south Louisiana and I was so excited about what the Lord spoke to me, that

I told the pastor—big mistake. I said, "You aren't going to believe this . . ." and I was right. He didn't believe it.

I said, "Guess what?"

He said, "What?"

"The Lord said He's gonna give me a jet!" I said.

That pastor looked at me like, *Stupid boy, stupid fool.* He said, "You can't even fill up a Toyota, how are you gonna get a jet?"

Now, it was true for the time—for my situation—but it hurt me to hear it. God had just lifted me up; this pastor had just tried to tear me down. The man kind of hurt my feelings. Although I didn't show it, on the inside I thought to myself, *the old fool.* I decided to ignore what he said and just keep believing—it was the right thing to do.

You see, it's the person who's never done anything who's just sure nothing can be done! There is a Scripture in Matthew 7:6 that says, *"Give not that which is holy unto the dogs, neither cast ye your pearls before swine, lest they trample them under their feet, and turn again and rend you."*

When I shared what God told me with that pastor, I didn't realize that he couldn't believe with me, that it was too big for him to receive by faith. And, in effect, by telling him what God said, I was casting my "pearl" before someone who could not recognize the value of it.

Now, at that time, I didn't have enough finances coming into the ministry to fill up my ten-gallon gas tank, much less a jet—but that was beside the point. God was working on something in *me.* He was making a crack in my self-made limitations. He was showing me my future as a worldwide evangelist for Christ, at a time when my scope was limited to the southeastern United States.

When that jet flew over, God gave me the picture in my head and the words in my spirit that started to propel my faith to a higher level—to get me thinking about reaching more people for Christ. He was pushing my faith, giving me a goal, so that I could start building a mental map on the road to divine destiny.

I reached the goal. Today, many years later, my ministry has a jet.

But when I think back, I realize that even then, time wasn't an issue. I knew it was coming. God said it. Now, could I bring God's words to me to pass on my own? No! But, God could.

Yes, it took me years to see that vision come to pass, but guess what? My ministry has grown and today, the jet we're flying is not the first one we've had—glory! I use that thing to go to all my meetings, and I wear them out like most people wear out cars. I fly that much to preach the Gospel of Christ. Airlines can't even fly my schedule; I hop from one city to the next, night after night, all over the world.

My point is simply this: **God can do anything, and you will always have someone that dismisses your dream.** There are far more pessimists than optimists in the world—and even fewer of the optimistic, faith-filled, Christians. So, if you know you're talking to someone who can't yet believe with you, don't share that pearl!

This is a spiritual concept. It's the power of resistance at work—resistance to falling into the trap of dealing with natural thinking and fleshly attitudes.

It is better to keep your dream to yourself when you're talking to pearl-stomping people. And if, like me, you end up sharing your heart with someone you think will encourage you, but doesn't, remind yourself not to do it again. Obviously they're just shortsighted in that area. They either don't understand or they're misled in some way.

Shrug it off as best as you can and remember that God has helped many people to do many great things on this earth . . . and you can bet that not one of those people got a nod of approval and a slap on the back every time they shared their thoughts and dreams with others.

CHAPTER 5

RUNNING TOWARD YOUR DESTINATION

I BELIEVE IN destiny. But to a lot of people, that word is one that only belongs in the "other worlds" of the silver screen. Try to remember the last time you talked about your destiny. If you bring it up at the dinner table, people will look at you like you've just been cast in the next George Lucas movie . . . like you're about to shrink down to eighteen inches, turn green like Yoda, and start saying, "Faith, I am!"

In today's world, *destiny* is a word that isn't used too much because it's lofty and can seem "beyond" us. But let me tell you something . . . destiny is real. Every day, people just like you are living out their destiny all around the world. They might not be flipping a glowing laser sword around, but they are using the Sword of the Spirit and moving through their lives with something way more effective—faith!

We've all got a destination. We've all got a destiny. Some people have seemingly "larger" destinations to reach than others, but all of us are important. We've all got something to do that matters, whether it appears that way or not. If you just touch one person in this world and help him along in some way, it's worth it.

Some people are running toward their destiny by teaching children in a classroom. They are opening minds and teaching future generations. Others are running toward their destiny by creating new and helpful things for the public's use. They are inventing methods and objects that will change the way our world works! Still others are running toward their destiny simply by helping *others* to fulfill their dreams. They are the champions of dreams that can only get done with team effort.

We all have a place in this world—a destiny to achieve and a destination to reach. It's a place rooted in goodness that, I believe, we should run toward in godly faith.

DESTINY BEYOND THE ANIMAL SPECIES

I'm a big fan of nature TV. Although I'm a Cajun from south Louisiana in America, for years my house was filled with the sounds of an English accent . . . I'm talking about the narrators of *Wild Kingdom*! For some reason or another, only the English seemed to get those narration jobs. Not once did I hear a Cajun saying, "Now, dis the blue whale and he big! Coouleee, look at 'em go down der deep!" No, the narrators of those shows always made sure to sound refined and whispery, and excitement was kept to a minimum on the plains of Africa.

Cathy would get tired of watching those poor wildebeests bite the dust when the lions came to town, and she'd say, "When are you going to change the channel?" She didn't like to see the blood and guts, but I loved it. When I watched the lions hunt and the elephants trumpet, I felt like I was there—a Cajun smack-dab in the middle of *Wild Kingdom*!

Sure enough, at some point in nature TV programs, I would hear the word *destiny*. One program would talk about the destiny of the blue whale. Another about the destiny of the Asian elephant or the gray wolf. They'd talk about the destiny of some other exotic animal that they were just sure was on the verge of global extinction.

But, as I think about it today, I wonder, *What about the destiny of another species? Mankind! What about the destiny of the human soul?*

The destiny of the believer who truly walks by faith? Are they in danger of extinction, too?

DESTINED TO WALK BY FAITH

People are so busy with their own lives today. They're going to church, but their mind is on the afternoon football game. They're driving past people who need Jesus every day, but their mind is on stopping at the next fast-food joint for a burger. They may go right past someone who needs help because they are too busy thinking about themselves. Very few are thinking about their destiny, not just in terms of their occupation, but their destiny as a child of God.

It seems that there just aren't as many people who really hunger for God-like faith—the kind of faith that heals and moves mountainous problems into the sea. Think about it. How many people walking the earth today could be compared to the faith giants of yesteryear? Men like John G. Lake, Smith Wigglesworth, Charles Finney, and all those others who could be listed in "God's Faith Hall of Fame," if there were such a thing.

I love reading about the faith-filled men throughout history. They were not perfect and each was still a product of his time and generation, but they were fiercely committed to bringing the Gospel to the world and fiercely committed to their faith in God. What a destiny! Their hunger for God-like faith was insatiable, and it caused them to be men of great influence. They changed the world around them for the better.

Do you know what all those great faith-giants have in common? They're dead! That's right, they've all moved on to Heaven. So, who will be the faith giants of this generation? Who will grab the flaming torch handed down by our forefathers of faith and run with passion toward the mark? Who will stand up and say, "I'm not extinct! I'm right here and I'm ready to go ye into all the world and preach the Gospel to every creature! I'm ready to evangelize and support evangelism! I want to see people healed, saved, and set free by the power of God!"

Who will be the next faith-giant? It can be you. Well, it can if your faith has a destination. You might say, "A destination? What do you mean by that, Brother Jesse?" I mean that you'll never fulfill God's plan for your life if your faith doesn't have a destination—a place set for the end of your life's journey. Think finish line!

Many believers would love to have lived the lives of some of the men mentioned above. They admire such loyal commitment to God, and they would love to be just like them, seeing miraculous acts of faith and power service after service. Yet, as much as some believers admire others, many seem to go through their Christian lives with only one destination in mind—to *have* faith.

Faith is not your destination. It's not the finish line. It's the beginning line. You don't have to spend years trying to attain faith. Faith isn't a gold medal. It isn't even a prize.

Faith is like the perfect pair of running shoes. It's going to get you to the finish line quicker than running barefoot ever would! Faith is what will carry you to your destination. It's the supernatural force that gives you the help and endurance you need to go through life at a strong, steady pace.

Faith—It's what helps you to do the works that Jesus did
    and greater.
Faith—It's what is going to help you press toward the
    mark of your calling in life.
Faith—It's what is going to help you finish your course
    with joy!

Faith is the action that will carry you to your destination. That is, if you have a destination in mind.

IF YOU DON'T KNOW WHERE YOU'RE GOING, YOU WON'T KNOW WHEN YOU GET THERE

The bottom line is this: If you don't know where you're going, you're not going to know when you get there. You've got to have a finish line in mind. I'm not talking about a list of things you want to do before you die, although that's not a bad thing to have. But I'm talking about a goal in life, something to build your mental map toward.

Your goal could be as lofty as becoming the political leader of your country and creating change for millions. Or it could be as seemingly humble as simply helping someone in your community to not go hungry today.

Some have bigger visions than others but, together, we all fit and work according to God's plan. But it's up to us to follow Him, to follow that inner leading in our heart and His Word and reach our destination, whatever that destination may be.

If you don't know where you're going, you are going to need to start consciously praying about your life. Don't let it overwhelm you. Life doesn't happen all at once. It happens in minutes and hours. Take each day as another opportunity to seek God about what He would want for you to do that particular day.

When I get up in the morning, I talk to God first thing. I don't wait until something bad happens to communicate with God. I do it no matter what's happening.

Every morning, when you get up, make a conscious effort to pray. You can do it while you're still in bed. You can even do it while you're brushing your teeth. Don't let what's going on around you distract you. Talk to God, either out loud or inside. Ask Him to lead you by His Holy Spirit.

Each morning, ask God to open your eyes to the opportunities around you that day. Remember, your destiny happens one day at a time. I believe, with all my heart, that if you seek God, you will find His plan for your life. When you get that plan, you're going to be able to get determined about it. Your mental map will lead you from determined thoughts, to faith, to ideas, and then to action.

If you happen to get off track, all you have to do is go back to the original thought. What did God tell you or show you? What idea did He reveal to you? Go right back to wherever you went off track, and start there again. I don't care if it's been ten years. Go back. Do what you are supposed to do.

If you are a believer, remind yourself that you have hope and you're not alone. You don't have to "come up" with your own destiny. God has good plans already. You just have to follow His lead and notice what He's putting in front of you. But, you can't be led by Someone you never communicate with . . . so, make a conscious decision to start talking to God!

In Jeremiah 29:11–12 (Amplified Bible), God says, *"For I know the thoughts and plans that I have for you, says the Lord, thoughts and plans for welfare and peace and not for evil, to give you hope in your final outcome. Then you will call upon Me, and you will come and pray to Me, and I will hear and heed you."*

Now, I didn't start out in life following the Scriptures or doing things this way. I started out like a lot of people, figuring that I had to make my own way and make my own destiny, all on my own. I didn't have a concept that God could actually lead me or talk to my heart. I figured nobody was going to help me, but me.

OUT OF POVERTY, INTO A PLACE OF PLENTY

I was worried about having a goal in life when I was only five years old. That's one thing about being born into a dirt-poor family in Louisiana. You learn your lessons early. I distinctly remember being five years old and crying out to God. "God, I don't know what we're gonna do!"

On the heels of that cry, I had a thought. *One day I'll make a success of myself. Then Mama will have enough to eat. She'll have anything she wants to wear. One day!*

I determined my destiny when I was five years old. Where was I headed? Out! Out of my house. Out of poverty. Out of lack. Into a place of plenty . . . and I knew for sure that it wasn't in the bayous of south Louisiana.

How would I get there? I had no earthly idea, but I was going. My faith wasn't in God, it was in me, but still I had a destination—and that principle works no matter who you are.

You may have heard me say that I was a heathen by the age of eight. It's true. My mama told me so! Of course, it happened because of the commitment I made three years earlier. You see, I grew to hate prayer because I didn't believe God listened anyway. My mama would say, "Bow your head, Jesse!" I would do it, but it was just a motion to me.

You see, my natural disposition is about the bottom line. As a kid, I figured that things ought to be plain. I heard people at our church talk about God healing. But guess what? They were all sick. So, what they said meant nothing to me.

I knew people who believed God would bless them and preached it, too. You guessed it. They were all broke. They didn't believe what they were talking about. So, why should I? It was pointless to me, even at a very young age. I had no concept of God as a benevolent Father. To me, He was the guy in the sky with lightning bolts ready to throw them at you if you ticked Him off.

As a kid, I reasoned that if "he that endureth to the end will be saved," then I was just going to wait until the end. To me, there was no point going through anything you didn't have to. I was miserable enough as it was.

The Christians I knew had preacher barbecues every weekend that seemed open to the whole community. But if a black man made the mistake of walking into our church, he probably wouldn't have made it back out. That was the way it was in south Louisiana in the 1950s. By the time I was eight years old, I'd seen too much hatred and bigotry in God's name, and I didn't want any part of it.

My mother wasn't prejudiced, even though she attended a church filled with prejudiced people. I remember asking her, "Mama, what's the matter with the people at that church?"

"They're foolish," she said, sighing. "They're stupid. They shouldn't act that way."

After three years of waiting for God to show up, I gave up believing that He would. I was eight years old and made a declaration, "I don't believe in your God, Mama," I said.

"You're a heathen!" she gasped, slapping me.

"God don't do nothing!" I argued. Slap!

Mama's slapping and rebuking did no good. I gave up on God. I had a destination in my life and, by the age of eight, I figured I'd have to get there on my own. I wanted out of poverty, out of Louisiana, out of everything that I'd grown to hate.

It was especially important that I figure out what to do with my life, because I wasn't supposed to be. My daddy let me know that I was a fleeting moment of passion. "Boy," he said, "you sure caught us by surprise." It was the simple truth.

SURPRISE, SURPRISE, SURPRISE—VEIL BABY!

If the news of my imminent arrival took my parents by surprise, that was nothing compared to the jolt they got when I was born.

They tell me that, when they first looked at me, I didn't have any eyes. I didn't have a nose. I didn't have a mouth.

"My God, what is it?" my mother cried.

"Let's put it back," Daddy said.

"Well looky here!" the doctor said. "It's a veil baby!"

Veil baby? my daddy thought, *It better be a Duplantis baby!*

I was born with a piece of skin covering my face. Someone told me it happens about once in every thirty million births. I'm not sure if that is true, but that's what I've been told. Mama said the doctor clipped that skin away and I saw light for the first time.

There's something about being the middle child. Mama always worried about the oldest, and she always worried about the youngest.

"There's just something about you," Mama said. "I've got to take care of your brother. I've got to take care of your sister. You . . . you'll make it."

How will I make it? I wondered. Maybe like Daddy, in the oil field.

"Mama," I'd ask. "What am I gonna do?" In other words, what's my destiny?

"I don't know," she'd say thoughtfully. "But you won't be an oil field worker. You're going to do something different."

"What, Mama?"

"It'll be revealed."

MY DESTINY STARTED WITH MUSIC

The day I found out I could play a guitar was the day I knew I'd found my key out of poverty. I had no idea that playing music would actually give me tools for life that would help me in my true destiny as a minister of the Gospel, but it did.

While the other kids would be outside playing, I'd be in my room strumming that guitar. Learning music created a strong discipline in my life. I knew that I couldn't get good by doing it haphazardly. I had to hit that thing day after day after day. Today, my schedule as a minister is grueling and I've been at it full-time since 1976. I believe that the discipline that it takes to keep me moving today was birthed in me as a child, and it started with playing guitar as a very young boy.

My daddy showed me three chords and since he liked country music, I started off playing country music, which I never did like much. Then I discovered Elvis Presley, and it was like fire hit me. I wanted nothing but to rock-n-roll! I'd sing to myself in my room, "Hubba hubba hubba hub . . ." I'd play as loud as I could. I'd take my guitar and beat up the corners of the house, sliding it up and down, just to hear the noises I could make.

"Jesse!" Mama would holler, "Go outside and play!"

I'd go, but I'd take that old guitar with me. The man across the street would yell, "Hey! Little Jesse! Come over here and play for me!" I'd play every song I knew for him, which was three. He was so patient and kind. He applauded every time. This went on for years. Every time I played for him, he gave me a word of encouragement, which kept stirring me to play more.

"You can do anything you want!" he'd say. "You're an American!"

"Is that the same as being Cajun?" I asked.

"Play that guitar!" he'd say. "Play yourself out of here and into the world!"

Words like that go into a kid, especially when you get no encouragement at home. I believe God used that man to help me along in my destiny which was, eventually, to preach the Gospel. I learned early how just a few encouraging words can make all the difference. Today, when I preach, I know that there are many people in the audience who are down in the dumps and need uplifting. We all need hope, and hearing how bad we are isn't what's going to help us, right? You see, my destiny as a preacher was being cultivated in me, even then.

So, as a kid, I'd play that guitar. Eventually, I started playing other instruments too. Now, why did I practice, practice, practice when I could have been having fun? Because I had a destination, a goal to do something with my life. Another thing I did, because I wanted to make it out of my situation at home, was to make good grades. I figured the only way out of there was to work hard and make good grades. I was an oddity among the Duplantis clan. I don't use the word *clan* lightly. The Duplantis bunch was Catholic for a while and that meant no birth control. We grew into a clan and out of that clan of people, I believe that I'm one of the few who consistently made good grades.

I'm the only one who graduated from high school. Was I smarter than the rest? No, I just had a goal of getting out that drove me to be disciplined. I wanted something bad enough that I was willing to do what I had to do, and that is a key element in being successful whether it is spiritual, physical, or financial.

When I was eleven years old, Mama told me, "Son, I want you to play in church for the camp meeting they're having."

"Why would I want to do that?" I asked. "First, they don't pay. And second, they don't even appreciate good music."

But, as usual, Mama got her way and I went to the church on the night of the camp meeting to play my guitar. The leaders listened to me play a little before service. Then they asked me and a few others to get on the platform. They didn't have a place for us to sit, so we stood with our instruments.

Now, I had a habit when I played—I moved. When we started playing, I turned that guitar toward the amplifier, put in a few licks, and started moving. I couldn't help it. The music was in me and it was coming out of me . . . but I was in church, so it didn't go over too well. Suddenly, the sound went dead and I heard a voice yell from the pew, "Get that kid off there!" I looked and saw that they had just pulled the plug out of the socket. That was the first time I was thrown out of church.

"You can't play!" they said. "You've got devil music in you!" "And you've got some of that black music in you, too!"

I was flippant and said, "Yeah, well y'all need some black mamas in here! Them sorry fat white women can't sing a lick!" Oh, they were so mad, the spit was flying! So, I made a plan that would keep my destiny moving . . . I got out of that church!

A NEW DESTINATION

If you know me, you may know my personal testimony, so I won't get into it here. But, by the time I was in my early twenties, my talent had been honed. I had learned a lot about people and I could play music in my sleep. I'd sold my talent to the world. I was in a band, touring and making more money than I'd ever thought I'd make. I had it all by my own standards. I had enough money to buy whatever I wanted, when I wanted.

What made me walk away from it? Destiny.

There is a way that man goes in life—a way that he creates for himself—but it is fleeting and unfulfilling. Without God, even your greatest dream will one day feel empty and tired. That is what happened to me.

I got to a point in my life and in my career where there was no happiness at all. Music was nothing to me. It was just a way out of my childhood misery. It was my way to make money. I was strong-willed and strong-minded. I was full of bravado. I figured I had made it on my own and didn't need anybody else but me, but I was wrong. I was miserable.

You see, my mama didn't leave me alone. She prayed for me and prayed for me and prayed for me. Eventually her prayers and faith started working to bring me back to the altar of God. When you pray for someone else, you are using your own power and energy to affect them for good.

Mama knew that I was getting to a dead-end road. She knew that I needed God and she was right. You see, the moment I made the decision to reject God as a child was the moment my mama began to really intercede in prayer for me. Years went by, but eventually her destination and my destination met up. I gave my life to Christ after watching Billy Graham preach on television on Labor Day Weekend in 1974, and I did it right before I had to leave the hotel room to go and play a rock show.

That moment in the hotel room changed my destination in life.

After that, my direction in life wasn't fueled by the poverty of my youth. It wasn't fueled by my dysfunctional family or the hypocrites I saw growing up in church. It was fueled by a simple love for the One who first loved me—Jesus.

Love will change you. Love will take you from the place you thought you wanted to go, and redirect you to the place where you're meant to be.

My place was with the Lord Jesus Christ—not alone. My place was His house—not in some rat-infested nightclub. My place was, years later, His pulpit preaching the Gospel—not hitting the bass guitar, loaded up on drugs, and scanning the place for women.

I wasn't a good man, but God took me in. I thought only about myself, but He didn't let that deter Him from opening His arms to me. God took me when no one else would. But it took that decision, that moment of salvation and surrender—that moment of change—to redirect my steps in life and to find a new destiny, a new destination, a place that God had made, just for me.

THERE'S NOTHING INFECTIOUS ABOUT SECONDHAND FAITH

Why didn't I catch hold of the faith of those Christians that crossed my path when I was young? Why didn't I have a life-changing moment when I was young? Why did I have to go through so much sin to get to the place of salvation?

I believe it was because the people I saw as a young boy were trying to live off the faith of others. It was tradition to them. They may have been living off the truth of their mama's relationship with God. Maybe they were living off the faith of the founder of that church. Maybe they were trying to live off the faith of preachers of old.

It really doesn't matter. You see, secondhand faith isn't infectious. It's just a bunch of rules and regulations. I don't think I could catch real faith from them if I rubbed up against them all day. **The only antidote for secondhand faith is firsthand relationship.**

God doesn't want to take anything from us. He wants to give everything to us. He's not a taker, He's a giver. Anything He asks you to give or give up has one purpose—to make your life better, to open the door for you to receive more.

God didn't ask me to give up my musical career in a rock band. He didn't ask me to cut my long, 1970s hair or even stop doing drugs or drinking. He asked for my heart. He showed me His love. He showed me a path that was greater than the one I was walking on before.

I chose to leave the band because it was at odds with my new firsthand relationship with God. I chose to stop drinking and doing drugs because I no longer needed those things as a crutch in my life. Did I know where I was going in life after I met Jesus? No, I didn't! I didn't know what would become of me. I just knew that I *had* to follow after God.

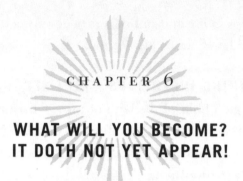

CHAPTER 6

WHAT WILL YOU BECOME? IT DOTH NOT YET APPEAR!

*Behold, what manner of love the Father hath bestowed upon us, that we should be called the sons of God: therefore the world knoweth us not, because it knew Him not. Beloved, now are we the sons of God, and **it doth not yet appear what we shall be**. . . .*

1 JOHN 3:1–2

IT MAY NOT yet appear what you will be. When you accept Christ as your Savior, you're on a new path. You begin a new destiny—and everything that happened to you in the past becomes a steppingstone to your future good life.

You see, I don't believe it was God's will for me to go through everything I went through as a young man. But I do believe that, even in my own choices to live life my own way—which was often against His way—I was learning things that would actually help me in my destiny as a preacher.

God gave me the talent to play music. Church people used me.

Some cut my talent down and didn't want me to move the body God gave me. So, I left. I went elsewhere. Was that God's will? I don't think so! It was people saying cruel things, doing cruel things, and not encouraging me to stick with God. They threw me out of church, not God! Sometimes Christians can ruin Christianity if you let them!

Look, the talent God gave me for music became a steppingstone in my destiny to be a minister because I learned a lot in my years as a musician. Just standing on stage and playing in front of a crowd taught me things. I learned how to gauge an audience, how my actions produced their reactions. I learned what to do when I bombed. I learned how to be self-employed, how to work with others, and how to run a business. I learned that what I did on that stage could stimulate others' thinking. All of that helped me as I made my way toward my true destiny.

You may not have gotten as far away from your God-intended path as I did. You may not need a huge career change like I did. But, one thing is for certain, if you have made Jesus the Lord of your life, change is coming, and everything you experienced in the past can be used as a learning tool toward your future. Even if it is simply what *not* to do anymore!

Everything changes when you start following God, but it ALL starts on the inside first. **Jesus was a fisher of men, but He didn't try and clean the fish before He caught them.** He dealt with the heart, the place where change is supposed to happen first.

So, what will you become? Maybe it doth not yet appear! Don't worry about it. Just follow after God and He will start to show you how to begin walking on this new path with Him. If your heart is open, He will give you dreams, ideas, and concepts that have the potential of becoming mental maps on the road of destiny.

To me, 1 John 3:1–2 makes it clear that not only should we be *called* the sons of God, we *are* the sons of God. But, do you know what gets folks really riled up? People get mad when I say I'm a son of God. They write me ugly letters.

But you know, it makes no difference to me whether somebody believes that God has adopted me into His family or not. I know He has! Nobody can take this salvation away from me.

One Catholic lady asked me, "Are you a saint?"

"Yes," I told her.

"When did they canonize you?" she asked.

"When I was born again."

I know we're using different terminology because every denomination and religion has its own lexicon but, you know, the Word of God says that I've been made the righteousness of Christ Jesus. So, in that sense, I am a saint. I'm pure in His sight. If I do something wrong, I ask forgiveness and the blood of Jesus washes me clean of all unrighteousness.

Of course, you and I are not *the* Son of God, but according to the Bible, we are sons and daughters of God. We are joint-heirs with Christ Jesus and heirs to the promises of God. Galatians 3:29 says, *"And if ye be Christ's, then are ye Abraham's seed, and heirs according to the promise."*

"Why is that so important, Brother Jesse?" someone asked.

Well, it's simple. You have to know in Whom you have believed! You must have a firsthand relationship with Christ that causes you to want to give it all to Him—to have faith in Him for whatever comes your way.

Verse two in 1 John 3 says it all. *"It doth not yet appear what we shall be. . . ."*

That means that we are not finished products. What will we be like next week? What about next year? It doth not yet appear. But, I can tell you one thing. If you're the same, you're not going anywhere. Why? Because your faith doesn't have a destination. If it did, you would have moved toward it.

I can hardly wait to see what I'll look like next year. But it doth not yet appear, even though I look in the mirror every day. I love to read the Word of God aloud. Why? Because faith comes by hearing and not by reading. I've got to have faith to reach my destination. So, I read along and substitute my name in those Scriptures because God is talking to me.

I was doing that one day when the devil interrupted me. "Do you think all those words in the Bible belong to you?"

I answered without thinking. "No, devil, two of them belong to you. All the rest belong to me."

The devil is so stupid, he asked, "Which two belong to me?"

"Your words are *The End!* All the rest belong to me!"

You see, I know who I am in Christ. I've been redeemed by the blood of the Lamb. I'm more than a conqueror. If God be for me, who can be against me? If the Word says that I can have it, then why not believe for it?

MAN SUCCEEDS BECAUSE HE THINKS HE CAN AND FAILS BECAUSE HE BELIEVES HE WILL

Too often, people fall in love with God, but divorce His Word from their life. You can't do that and succeed with God. It's like shooting yourself in the foot before you ever get running in the race!

> *In the beginning was the Word, and the Word was with God, and the Word was God.*
> *The same was in the beginning with God.*
> *All things were made by Him; and without Him was not any thing made that was made.*
> *In Him was life; and the life was the light of men.*
> *And the light shineth in darkness; and the darkness comprehended it not.*
>
> *JOHN 1:1–5*

When people try to divorce the Word of God from their life, they've turned out all the lights. They've blinded themselves. If you could see into the Spirit realm, a lot of Christians would look like veil babies. They're wandering around trying to reach their destination with no real light and no real vision. In reality, they're trying to finish their race, but they've wandered off the course!

If you want to be on the right path, you need light. That light is a relationship with God.

John 1:5 says that God is the light that shines in the darkness, but those that walk in the darkness don't understand God. So, if you want to know more about God, read His Word. Get to know His nature as a good God. It will revolutionize your life. It will inspire you in the basics of life. Then it will inspire you to expand your thinking, which will, in turn, give you determined thoughts, which will produce ideas. Then you will be motivated to take action, which will draw you into your destiny.

Jesus made it pretty plain in John 14:15 when He said, *"If ye love Me, keep My commandments."* In other words, "Read My book." After all, how can you obey God if you don't know what He says?

God is one with His Word and when you get one with His Word, it's going to change the way you think. Therefore, it'll change the way you act, and eventually the path of your life will turn toward your destiny.

Success starts in the mind. As they say, man succeeds because he thinks he can. Man fails because he believes he will. The Word of God will help you to succeed spiritually, physically, and financially, but it all starts with what you believe.

Let's just face it, when you know God is backing you, it's easier to move forward. When you know God is with you, it's easier not to fear the future. When you know that God loves you, it's easier to go for the good things in life.

How does believing in yourself and what you're doing fit in with mental mapping? It's simple. You need people to make the ideas, dreams, and concepts God has given you come to pass. Nobody is an island. We need people to make anything happen. Remember my worldwide television story? God told me that He was going to put me on worldwide television. Did He beam a picture of me preaching into the sky? No. He used people.

People got behind the vision. People gave toward the vision. People helped me film the first shows and aired them. Then, people at TBN saw the local show. Somebody decided that I would be good for their network. Somebody faxed the contract. Somebody offered me the free airtime on worldwide television. I know I'm beating this into the ground, but I want you to get this . . . I needed people to help fulfill the vision God gave me, and you will need people to help you fulfill the vision God gave you, too.

You can't do it alone. So, if you need other people's help, then you need to be able to share your vision in a confident way. You have to believe in yourself. If you don't, it may be that nobody else will either! You can't get anybody to believe in you, if you don't.

Leaders lead by getting others interested in following. Think of it this way. If God gave you a dream, an idea, or a vision of your future, you've got to convince yourself that God can't lie. What He gave you is worth pursuing. It's worth being confident about. It's worth involving others in the dream, too. If you don't involve other people, you aren't a leader, you're a loner—and it's hard to get things done without people.

THEY WERE CLEANSED "AS THEY WENT"

God wants you healthy, happy, prosperous, and with a mind toward helping others. I meet a lot of people as I travel, but I don't listen too much to people who say, "Well, you know, Brother Jesse, the last time I was sick, it was pretty bad. I felt like . . ."

I interrupt and say, "I don't want to hear that."

"Huh?"

"Don't rehearse what the devil did! Rehearse what Jesus has done!"

"But I'm sick!" they say.

"Well, by Jesus's stripes you're healed! Take 'I am healed' and omit 'I am sick.'"

"How long would that take, Brother Jesse?"

"Do you ask that question when you take cold medicine? Do you ask it when you take a tablet for a headache? Do you feel better as soon as you take it? No. You have to wait for it to kick in. About twenty or thirty minutes later, your sinus passages will open up and suddenly you can breathe again."

"See, Brother Jesse, you said it yourself. Cold medicine works quickly."

"Yeah, but there's one big difference. Those cold remedies never conquered a cold. They just dull the symptoms of the sickness. They do nothing to help the actual problem. In about three hours, you'll be hacking and clacking again."

When you take a dose of Jesus's stripes, by faith, you aren't depending on just suppressing your symptoms; you're actually using the force of faith within you to receive healing, to draw on the power of what Christ did at Calvary.

"But He was wounded for our transgressions, He was bruised for our iniquities: the chastisement of our peace was upon Him; and with His stripes we are healed" (Isaiah 53:5).

Suppressing symptoms and being healed are two different things. Some people are spontaneously healed when they exercise their faith, but others are like the lepers Christ healed in the Bible—they receive their healing along the way.

> *And as He entered into a certain village, there met Him ten men that were lepers, which stood afar off:*
>
> *And they lifted up their voices, and said, Jesus, Master, have mercy on us.*
>
> *And when He saw them, He said unto them, Go shew yourselves unto the priests. And it came to pass, that, **as they went,** they were cleansed.*
>
> LUKE 17:12–14

When did they get healed? As they went! In other words, as they walked in obedience to what Jesus said, they were healed. It was birthed out of obedience, the action of walking based on faith in Christ's word.

As you walk by faith, you will be healed. As you walk by faith, you will gain insight into ways God wants to prosper you. As you walk by faith, you will make decisions that will lead you on the road to your divine destiny.

THE FEAR-KILLING POWER OF FELLOWSHIP

The more you obey God, the more you fellowship with Him, the more you are aware of your place in His body. The more you know who God is and who you are, the less you will fear the devil or even other people. There is a fear-killing power in having fellowship with the Father.

I'm quite sure of my future. I have the joy of my salvation. I have the safety of His favor. I have the inspiration of His Spirit. I'm in right-standing with God and that changes everything.

You see, if you have God in your life, when you start to run your race, you can do it with joy, knowing that you've already won. The trophy is already yours. You don't have to prove yourself to God. Jesus has already proven Himself.

"Brother Jesse, what if I don't know which way to go?"

Walk in His footsteps. Obey His Word. Start walking forward with an eye on obeying the two most simple and profound commandments of Christ.

And thou shalt love the Lord thy God with all thy heart, and with all thy soul, and with all thy mind, and with all thy strength: this is the first commandment.

And the second is like, namely this, Thou shalt love thy neighbour as thyself. There is none other commandment greater than these.

MARK 12:30–31

If you just start working on these, you will find that they take care of a lot of problems in life. They also give you direction and will put you on the path to your destination.

WHAT WILL YOU DO?

Jesus told us, *"Verily, verily, I say unto you, He that believeth on Me, the works that I do shall he do also; and greater works than these shall he do; because I go unto My Father"* (John 14:12).

In other words, "Go and do great works. Make my works part of your destiny." It's the destiny of every believer, not just the faith preachers of long ago, to do the works of Christ. Do you want to see God's plan for your life fulfilled? Then it's time to go beyond just trying to attain faith. It's time to start living in faith and doing the works of Christ!

Without faith, you won't be aware of your true destination. And, without a destination, you won't be able to have the motivation to move forward. You must give your faith a destination. After all, how will you know if you've gotten there if you don't know where you're going in the first place?!

What is the link between faith and mental mapping? Without faith in yourself, you can't move forward. Without faith in God, you can't go anywhere worth going! You see, without faith or strong belief, there is no determined thought! There is nothing that leads you to action.

Faith is crucial. It may not be the only thing in the Bible, but it is mixed up with everything in the Bible. Do a study for yourself and you'll see, you can't have love, grace, mercy, forgiveness, or anything else in the Word without faith of some kind. You don't need much. Jesus said that if you have faith that is as small as a mustard seed, you can move mountains (Matthew 17:20). So, don't sell yourself short by dismissing faith. It's one of the keys to fulfilling God's great plan for your life.

Today, you may be just a few steps into your destiny, but where will you be on destiny's path at this time next year? Will you win your city? Your state? A nation?

It doth not yet appear.

Will you empty a hospital? Transform a prison? Own a television station? Start a Bible School? Print books in other languages? Win your local community to Christ? Fund a ministry that is spreading the Gospel all over the world?

Just like hundreds of great men and women of faith before you, you have the power to create change in the lives of people. It isn't just a nice-sounding idea, it is your destiny. Whether they are people next door or people halfway across the world, it doesn't matter. The question is, are you doing the works of Christ?

You can begin where your great forefathers of faith left off. The flaming torch they ran so passionately with is being passed from one faith-generation to the next, and it is now being held out to you.

Will you leave this great faith to others? Or will you reach out and grab it with both hands? Don't spend another day wondering what you should do with your life. Give your faith a destination. Grab that torch and begin to run toward your destiny!

CHAPTER 7

THE POWER OF WISE WORDS AND RIGHT CHOICES

PROVERBS IS CALLED the book of wisdom for a reason. In every chapter in that book, you can read about the various ways *not* to be a fool! Fools don't enjoy the fullness of their destiny. Some don't even get on the right road. Others start going on the right road, but they get distracted and never get back out there. Others get to a successful place, but end up losing it in the end . . . because they go out and act like the fool!

I meet fools every day. I know they're fools because they tell me. They say, "Oh, you know how God is . . . sometimes He does and sometimes He don't!" I look at them right in the face and think, *You calling God a liar? You're a fool!*

Oh, I smile and then I give them some encouragement in the Word. I pray that they receive it and change. Otherwise, they're going to have a rougher time in life than they need to, and people like me are going to have to encounter their foolishness for years on end. It's enough to wear you out!

Fools shoot themselves in the foot right before they start a big race by popping off at the mouth in doubt. Fools cry and moan that God doesn't provide for them right after He gave them an opportunity to work. Fools lie all day to others and get mad when somebody else does the same thing to them. They think, *How can this be?* It's called reaping, buddy! Enjoy it!

Fools also speak doubt. They talk bad about God and themselves. They tear themselves down, even when, in their heart of hearts, they really want to do something for God. Take my advice. Read Proverbs, and for God's sake and yours, don't be a fool!

If you want to find and stick to the road that leads to your divine destiny, you're going to need wisdom, and that comes from God. James 1:5 says, *"If any of you lack wisdom, let him ask of God, that giveth to all men liberally, and upbraideth not; and it shall be given him."* Wisdom also comes from knowing who you are in Christ and speaking by faith, even when outward circumstances don't give you any assurance at all.

THE DANGERS OF "TELLING IT LIKE IT IS"

You can either tear yourself down or build yourself up. It's up to you. Choose to speak faith. If you don't "feel" it, don't let that get you into "telling it like it is." **People who always "tell it like it is" end up living exactly as they tell it.** Their faith is working—it's just taking them in the wrong direction.

You've got to "tell it like you want it to be" if you want your life to change and you want to progress—this is part of mental mapping. Let what is in your mind come out of your mouth. Determined thoughts should lead to determined words. So, speak to your future as if it is something tangible . . . and it will eventually become tangible. You will see that dream, idea, vision, or concept, or whatever God has put in your heart come to pass.

Is this optimism? No, it's faith. But it takes optimism to use faith, and that's a good thing. Optimism is underrated to the natural mind, but it's God's way of doing things to speak positive and speak life.

You're going to have many opportunities to quit—don't take any of them. Throughout the Bible, you can find examples of people who got what they needed from God because they refused to give up. The woman with the issue of blood is a famous one. The story is repeated in Matthew, Mark, and Luke, with Mark and Luke giving more detailed accounts (Matthew 9:20-22, Mark 5:25-34, Luke 8:43-48). There are many others. Research your Bible for them and you'll find that their stories are extremely encouraging.

What you'll see is that, many times, the words people spoke in those stories were an indicator of their faith. Let that be a lesson to you that the words you speak are very important. It's not the words you speak only when you're in church that matter. It's the words you speak to yourself *every* day that make the difference.

The Bible says that, *"You are snared by the words of your mouth; You are taken by the words of your mouth"* (Proverbs 6:2, NKJV). The devil may lay the trap, but it's you who can either walk into it or not. Watch your lips!

Satan may try and bombard you with negative thoughts and, if he does, realize that those thoughts aren't your thoughts. Speak the Word over yourself and say, "No, my thoughts are lovely, just, and pure—of good report! I'm not going to rehearse these doubt-filled thoughts because they aren't mine. I'm going to think on these things!"

> *Finally, brethren, whatsoever things are true, what-soever things are honest, whatsoever things are just, whatsoever things are pure, whatsoever things are lovely, whatsoever things are of good report; if there be any vir-tue, and if there be any praise, think on these things.*
>
> *Those things, which ye have both learned, and received, and heard, and seen in Me, do: and the God of peace shall be with you.*
>
> PHILIPPIANS 4:8–9

Doubtful thoughts don't come from the Lord, and they sure don't give you any peace. Good thoughts settle your soul. And, actually doing what you've *learned, received, heard,* and *seen* in Christ brings you great peace of mind.

So, if your mind replays negative thoughts about yourself over and over, recognize that those aren't your thoughts. That's a tactic of the devil to get you to speak doubt and give up on your destiny. It's what *he* thinks . . . and when did what the devil thinks matter? Look, it's what God thinks that really matters!

God is the one that made you and loved you so much that He sent His Son to die for you. Man, if that's not encouraging, I don't know what is! Don't let negative thoughts entrap you into throwing away your dream.

Anybody can quit. Many people do. But you're not destined to quit . . . you're destined to finish your race and win, not because you can do it all on your own, but because you've got Jesus Christ, the Hope of Glory, on your side.

THE POWER OF CHRIST IS IN YOU!

Have you accepted Jesus as your Lord? Then God is living within your heart and that means His presence is *with* you and *in* you. You have a divine destiny in God. Wherever you go, He goes. If you mess up and steer off the righteous road, God is still with you. He loves you, no matter what you've done, and He wants to help you right where you are.

If you're in jail today, God is in jail with you. He isn't leaving until you do. He will go where you go and stay where you stay. As long as you repent and ask His forgiveness, His power and presence is there with you. He will be merciful to you. He will honor your recognition of Him and move according to your faith in His Word. You are never alone.

Wherever God goes, He leaves a trail of life, love, and confidence. As you stir up His Word in your own mind and mouth, you are tapping into His power within you and that will have an effect on you. You'll start leaving a trail of life, love, and confidence wherever you go, too.

Good words and good works will follow you, just like they followed Jesus. You'll have an inner knowing of what to do and when to do it—the peaceful guidance of the Holy Spirit at work. You will be on the right road to fulfilling your divine destiny.

In other words, Jesus doesn't have to be physically on the earth to continue doing great works because He left you with enough power to do the works He did, and even greater (John 14:12).

The power of Christ in *YOU* will *do* what the presence of Christ did when He walked the earth. Jesus spoke the truth in love. He was a giver and an encourager. He cared for people and had compassion. He was in touch with the Father and worked miracles through His faith. He left us not just stories of power, but real power that we can use every day.

Jesus also left you His peace. He said, "*. . . My peace I give unto you: not as the world giveth . . .*" (John 14:27). Jesus wasn't talking about the kind of peace the world speaks of, which is temporal and based on emotions. Jesus was talking about a higher peace—His peace and inner strength that comes from knowing that God is with you always.

His peace passes ALL understanding and it's available to every believer. Don't get mad at me if I've decided to take it! I know that worry is at odds with fulfilling my destiny and so, I don't want to do it!

SAY, SAITH, AND SAITH

Jesus didn't die on the cross and save you from your sins so that you could live a miserable and unfulfilled life. No, He came and shed His blood so that you could have life and have it in abundance, to the fullest, as John 10:10 says—so that you could have the power to put the devil in his place, under your blood-bought feet!

You've been purchased with a high price. 1 Corinthians 6:20 says, "*For ye are bought with a price: therefore glorify God in your body, and in your spirit, which are God's.*"

Ephesians 1:7–9 says, *"In Whom we have redemption through His blood, the forgiveness of sins, according to the riches of His grace; Wherein He hath abounded toward us in all wisdom and prudence; Having made known unto us the mystery of His will, according to His good pleasure which He hath purposed in Himself."*

Because of what Jesus did on the cross, you have access to God. You can take the Scriptures and speak them over your life and build mental maps that will draw you straight into God's good plan for your life—glory, I'm starting to preach! You can know His will for your life and do it!

Remember that God created you, and He is the one Who put the dreams and visions for your life in your heart. Don't let the devil lie to you and tell you that you "can't" or you "never will."

You are made in God's image, adopted into the family of God, and you can do *anything* with God's help. The devil is a liar. But, you've got to build that mental map, cast down any thought that would try and rise up against what the Word of God says and move forward (2 Corinthians 10:4–5).

Jesus told us to use our mouth in faith when He said, *"For verily I say unto you, That whosoever shall **say** unto this mountain, Be thou removed, and be thou cast into the sea; and shall **not doubt** in his heart, but shall **believe** that those things **which he saith** shall come to pass; he shall **have** whatsoever he **saith**"* (Mark 11:23).

Three times in the same verse we learn that our words matter, once to *believe*, once to *not doubt* but three times to *say, saith,* and *saith!* That's instruction straight from the lips of Jesus, and it ought to tell you something. Let the elevator go to the top!

WILL THE DEVIL FIGHT YOUR DREAM?

You better know he will! He fought God's dream to bring salvation to mankind. So, you can take it to the bank that he's going to try and fight your dreams, too, especially if he thinks you can actually do them!

You have to get beyond the boy with faith to confuse him. When you live by faith, he doesn't know what to do, but that doesn't mean he'll leave you alone. He's going to try and mess up your goals by trying to mess up your mental map. He wants to pollute your thought-life so that he can render you powerless to change. Don't let him.

He's going to try and pull on your flesh, tempt you to go off course in your spirituality. Remember that the flesh is all he's got to work with. As I mentioned earlier, he's a flesh-devil, not a faith-devil.

How can you use mental mapping as a tool to defeat the devil? Don't allow him to have a place in your thought-life. Refuse to dwell on his negativity. Instead, lean on the Word. If he tries to use somebody else's defeating words to drag you down, recognize it for what it is and don't accept it. Then, quote a Scripture to yourself or remind yourself of what God has already told you.

Remember that the devil can only work in the realm of the senses. You work in the realm of the spirit as well as the senses. The devil is a flesh-based tempter. His goal is to get you to quit and give up on God's good plan for your life. Whether it is spiritual, physical, emotional, or financial, he wants to render you powerless to do what you're meant to do in this life. But, he's only going to use the senses to tempt you.

After all, have you ever really been tempted in the Spirit? Think about it. Have you ever been tempted to tithe? I mean, were you under *heavy* temptation to give ten percent to the Lord? No! Do you know why? Tithing is a spiritual concept. You're only tempted in the flesh. Yet, the Lord said if you crucify your flesh (daily, instead of just on Sunday), you won't fulfill the lust of the flesh (Galatians 2:20).

In other words, putting God first every day is going to help you fulfill your dream, and sticking to your spirituality is going to help you stay on course.

BORN OF WOMAN'S SEED

God had a mental map, too. He chose the birth, life, death, and resurrection of Jesus Christ as His plan for man's redemption. He *saw* it with the eyes of faith and *spoke* that plan into existence, which was *evidence* to Him—a done deal—of what would come to pass. He did this all before we or the devil ever saw it actually happen. His mental map is also, of course, His Word. When we use His map to govern our map, we can be sure we're going in the right direction. His Word is final authority. When it becomes our final authority, we can only win.

God's map leads all the way to Heaven—a place with no sickness, no disease, no fear, no hatred, no malice . . . a perfectly joy-filled and peaceful place. It is what God wants for all of us to experience. But first, we have to live through this life, which is filled with all sorts of obstacles, some of which can hinder our goals.

The devil is spiritually dead in that, when he rose up against God, he lost his connection to God and became blind to God's way of doing things. That's what rejection of God does. It's why he's blind to spiritual concepts.

If the devil could grasp spiritual concepts like faith, he'd have an advantage. He doesn't. That's why he was so nervous after the fall of man. He knew he was at a disadvantage because, as a spiritually dead being, all he could go by was what he could *see* God do.

By the time the devil actually saw Christ born, he wasn't really all that sure if He *was* the Son of God. He had a king send spies to kill the baby Jesus, just in case, and the king passed a law to slay every child under the age of two.

Why wasn't he sure about Jesus? You have to remember, he's an old devil and Jesus didn't show up until a little over two thousand years ago, so he had a lot of years of trying to find "The One."

You see, the devil remembered those prophetic words of Jehovah God right after the fall of man: *"And I will put enmity between you and the woman, and between your seed and her Seed; He shall bruise your head, and you shall bruise His heel"* (Genesis 3:15, NKJV).

When the devil heard that, he totally misinterpreted it. It looks as if he thought, *Woman's seed? Well, anybody born of a woman, I can cause to fall. No problem.* Looking at his track record in the Word, we can see that he went to work on many people that he saw as a threat.

The problem was that God was talking about something altogether different and spiritual—The Immaculate Conception—because *women* don't have seed; men have seed. Nobody can be born of "woman's seed" unless a miracle happens. Ladies, you need us men for something!

Yet, from the moment the devil heard God's promise in Genesis 3:15, he thought the Messiah would come soon. So, he worked on Cain to kill Abel, the first man that the devil considered "good" and maybe "The One." Prophet after prophet and good man after good man, the devil attacked. He was always on the lookout and did everything he could to steal, kill, and destroy God's people over the years.

By the time the true Messiah arrived on the scene, the devil was confused and didn't know if Jesus was just another prophet. You can tell this because when he tempted Jesus in the wilderness, he started with a question, "*. . . **If** thou be the Son of God, command that these stones be made bread*" (Matthew 4:3). He didn't know! And, to top it, he asked Jesus to do something he could *see*.

This is a foundational principle in building a mental map on the road to divine destiny. You need to realize that **your battles will be won in the spirit** and not in the flesh. You're going to **win in your mind before you win in the natural world.** It may seem unusual, but this is truly the way things work with God.

THE POWER OF RESISTANCE AT WORK

Now, I want you to think about what Jesus said to the devil when He was tempted. He didn't take the challenge to turn the stone into bread, even though He could do it.

Jesus could have turned that whole mountain into a loaf of bread with a log of butter running down the valley. Instead, He spoke the Word of God to Him: "*But He answered and said, 'It is written, Man shall not live by bread alone, but by every word that proceedeth out of the mouth of God'*" (Matthew 4:4).

Notice it! See it! Jesus refused to do something that the devil could *see*. He chose to *say* something spiritual—something the devil couldn't understand. In other words, **Jesus was not going to fight the devil. He chose to fight the good fight of faith.** He wasn't going to enter into a contest of miracle-working power. He was going to *say* only what God said—He chose to live by it!

When you're tempted to do something that would take you on a path that is at odds with your dream or vision, and you will be, remember . . . don't fight the devil; fight the good fight of faith. Exercise the power of resistance and speak the Word. Then, don't dwell on the temptation. Move on.

In the end, the devil lost royally to the King of Kings, and God's mental map manifested and gave all of us a future and a hope. The Scriptures tell us what the devil and his cohorts felt like after Jesus's death and resurrection: *"Which none of the princes of this world knew:* ***for had they known it, they would not have crucified the Lord of glory"*** (1 Corinthians 2:8).

They wouldn't have crucified Him if they'd known that, in doing so, they were slamming the nails into their own coffins and making a way for every believer, including you, to walk in the power of Christ.

Jesus said it best: ***"Verily, verily, I say unto you, He that believeth on Me, the works that I do shall he do also; and greater works than these shall he do; because I go unto My Father"*** (John 14:12).

Jesus is with the Father in Heaven today. He fulfilled His divine destiny and because He resisted the urge to quit or change course, you have the ability to be saved and do great works for God. So, what are you going to do? The ball is in your court. It's time to forget what lies behind you—past mistakes and problems—and press forward in faith to what lies ahead!

One of my all-time favorite Scripture passages is in Philippians 3:13–14: *"Brethren, I count not myself to have apprehended: but this one thing I do, forgetting those things which are behind, and reaching forth unto those things which are before, I press toward the mark for the prize of the high calling of God in Christ Jesus."* I love these verses. Speaking them over myself helps keep my mind focused on moving forward in my destiny.

A REPORT IS BEING MADE ON YOU

Every time you choose life, death, blessing, or cursing, somebody's recording it. Every time you have faith, help someone, love someone, or give time or finances toward good works, the books are being kept!

Hebrews 11:1, *"Now faith is the substance of things hoped for, the evidence of things not seen"* is followed by a verse that says, *"For by it the elders obtained a good report."* There is a report in Heaven being made about you.

You've got one life on this earth to live. After that, you're going to get your report card from on High. Will you get a good report like the elders of faith? I believe you will! If you're living by faith, you are pleasing to God. Hebrews 11:6 says, *"But without faith it is impossible to please Him: for he that cometh to God must believe that He is, and that He is a rewarder of them that diligently seek Him."*

It is more interesting and adventurous to live by faith. Plus, God rewards the diligent, and it takes diligence to build mental maps on the road to divine destiny. Your efforts won't be in vain and, in the end, you'll actually find that your destiny comes with more blessings. It's God's reward system in effect!

When you seek to fulfill your destiny, you're really seeking God. That plan for your life didn't originate with yourself; it originated with Him. He's the Creator and you are the co-creator of your own life. You *choose* to create your life *within* His life.

CHAPTER 8

A VISION OF SOMETHING BIGGER THAN "TODAY"

You've got places to go and people to touch! How are you going to get there? Vision!

Trusting God and moving in the direction of His will for your life is part of seeing that vision come to pass. Trusting in God is what it takes to get from point A to point B in your destiny. Today's journey should become a steppingstone toward tomorrow's dream. But, to realize that, you must have a vision of something bigger than "today."

Living "in the moment" is a good thing. You are meant to enjoy this life, day by day. You can only work for so many hours. Then you have to lay your head to rest on the pillow. But to reach a goal in your life, you will have to both live in the moment *and* have faith for the future.

Yes, if you follow after God day by day, you will fulfill your destiny and reach your destination. But if you open your mind to what can be and build a mental map about it, you're going to have greater hope and joy for the future. You'll look forward to getting up in the morning, knowing that each day is another opportunity to do something for God and move along destiny's path.

It's important to both enjoy life today and look forward to tomorrow, not worrying about tomorrow, but looking forward to it! There's a difference. Jesus told us not to be worried about the future because each day has enough trouble of its own (Matthew 6:34). He didn't say that we shouldn't think about the future, just don't worry about it.

I don't worry about anything. When I wake up in the morning, I don't dread the day. Why? Because I determine my destiny. I determine if I'm going to be aggravated or at peace, joyful or miserable. My attitude is up to me. You see, the devil may fight me, but he can't win because my trust is in the Lord! So, I'm sticking it out, no matter what, knowing that what I set my mind to do, I *will* do. It's just a matter of faith and time.

THREE-YEAR-OLD MOTOCROSS CHAMPION?

You may ask, "Well, Brother Jesse, why does it take so long to get things done?" Well, patience is required for success. **A delay is not a denial. Just because you *feel* stalled doesn't mean that you *are* stalled. The Lord works in mysterious ways, and, sometimes, we ask for things that we can't yet handle.**

A child can ask for a full-sized motorcycle at three years old, but it doesn't mean he should have it. But he can ask for it. He's able to dream about it and even start building his mental map, but it's not his time yet to ride that level of machine.

Now, it may be that child's destiny to become a motocross champion. He needs to start with something small and move up, bit by bit. If he's trained, he can become a champion by sixteen years old—but to win, he won't start out riding a champ's bike. That is for his future.

Well, you can ask God for many things that you can't yet receive. It is not that He is saying no to your requests, but He may delay what you ask for until you get "old enough" to receive it.

If you are a parent, you'll do the same thing with your children. You don't want to withhold anything good from them, but sometimes they can ask for something that they can't receive. If you gave it to them, they'd love to have it, but they wouldn't yet know how to handle it.

LONG-TERM GOALS, SHORT-TERM DELAYS

It's not easy when delays come up. It is natural to feel discouraged. But if you have faith that God is in control and that He is working it out, then you will have the inner strength needed to make it through the growing time—trust is a tool of mental mapping.

Another tool is simply reminding yourself each day of your long-term goal. Don't let it slip from your mental map. **Long-term goals will help to keep you from being frustrated by short-term delays.**

Delays come. It's a fact of life. But a delay is not a denial. If you stay focused on the long-term goal, you'll make it through the short-term delay.

We are all growing spiritually, and delays actually strengthen us because they help to develop patience in our lives. Nobody wants patience! We all want things now, but patience is a fruit of the Spirit, and it is required if you want to reach your long-term goals. Patience is another tool of mental mapping that will draw you into your divine destiny. It's not "doing nothing"—patience is actually an action. It is definitely something you have to work at!

People ask my wife, Cathy, all the time, "Does he ever get disappointed or discouraged?" They see me smiling in good times and in bad times and think I'm never disappointed or discouraged . . . and guess what? They're nearly right! I'm human and while my natural mind wants to fall into discouragement sometimes, I made a decision a long time ago to simply trust God.

I refuse to get down in the dumps when things are going slowly, because I already know what God can do. I've seen Him move on my behalf in the past, so I know that He will move on my behalf in the present and in the future. So, I refuse to bend to the pressure of time.

Time is on *my* side. Whatever stumbling blocks come up, God will help me to either move them out of my way or make it through them with joy—just knowing this is another tool that will help me to move my mental map into manifestation.

During all that time, I remind myself that I'm growing spiritually and I'm still moving forward—even if it is just spiritually and mentally. When the right time comes, I will have what is on my mental map physically. I just have to continue with persistence and patience—it's part of doing what it takes to get where I want to be in my life.

With God, I can't lose. That's my mentality when it comes to delays. I refuse to fall into the trap of disappointment and discouragement. When it looks like *nothing* is happening, something is happening—I'm growing in patience and honing my persistence skills.

THE BREAD OF FREEDOM, THE CUP OF VICTORY

When you have tasted the bread of freedom and drunk from the cup of victory, you're less likely to quit! What am I saying? Remind yourself of your past victories in life—this is a tool of mental mapping that will help you when you get discouraged by delays. Retaste the bread of your freedom and the cup of your victory. Do this especially when things aren't going the way you think they should go.

To avoid getting stuck in a rut of discouragement, stop and remind yourself of what God has already done in your life. Relive that victory. Consider it part of reviving your mental map. Doing this is going to remind you of what God can do. It's going to help you to resist the devil when he comes to try and discourage you.

Retasting your past victories is a way to get over the hump called "delays."

You see, sometimes delays are not happening just because the timing is off. Many times, delays are simply the work of that stinking devil from Hell who is working hard to hinder your success. He's trying to rob you of your destiny, either by discouragement, delays, or plain attacks against what you're doing. In that case, you can shut that boy down and speed the process back up by turning, fighting him in the spirit, and not in the flesh.

First, you have to retrain your mind to see the devil for what he really is—the loser. I find that a lot of Christians don't understand that the devil is just a little irritation. He may roar like a lion, but he's no lion. He may attack as if he's in control, but he's not in control.

The devil is not nearly as "big" as people make him out to be. Every day since he was kicked out of Heaven, he's been shrinking in power and ability. That's what happens when you're separated from the Source of Life—the Creator, God. In fact, the Bible tells us that at the end of time, we will see him and say, "Is *this* what caused all the trouble?"

Jesus conquered and put that idiot under your blood-bought feet! When you are obedient to Christ and put Him first in your life, you can *expect* that the devil will fight you. He wants to shut you down for one reason—to make the Gospel of no effect. His enemy is not you, it is God. But as God's child, you are reason enough for him to attack. When you know this, it's easier to stop whining about the attacks of the enemy on your life and start using the Word of God, in faith, so that you can get your mind refocused on your future.

Jesus called the devil a thief that comes only to kill, steal, and destroy. It's our job to enforce his defeat by rebuking and resisting him and putting our attention and faith in God. Jesus came to give us an abundant life, an overcoming life.

The battle Satan is waging may not have been your choice, but the outcome of that battle is. Jesus won at the cross and now, you just have to enforce that devil's defeat, glory! Don't buckle to the pressure. Realize that he is a fool and, while he may be able to hinder you, he can't stop you. God is on your side.

Use the Word as a spiritual sword and quote it in faith. Remind yourself of your past victories. It's a tool that you can use to regain confidence, renew patience, and refocus on the mental map that is leading you on the road to your destiny.

WHO ARE YOU BECOMING IN THE PROCESS?

This life is not only about where you're going, but it's also about *who* you are becoming along the way. The more **obedient** you are to God and the more **trust** you have in God, the more of your divine destiny you're fulfilling. The more **patient** and **faithful** you are, the more of your divine destiny you're fulfilling.

Hebrews 6:12 says, *"That ye be not slothful, but followers of them who through faith and patience inherit the promises."* If you want God's promises to you to be fulfilled, it takes both patience and faith, traits that don't fit in with laziness.

So, realize that, if you are sticking it out in faith and patience, you are literally using tools that will strengthen your mental map and lead you farther along in your destiny. James 1:3–4 says, *"Knowing this, that the trying of your faith worketh patience. But let patience have her perfect work, that ye may be perfect and entire, wanting nothing."*

Everybody wants to get to the place of "wanting nothing." But, with God, the road to that place is paved with patience. So, patience not only brings God's promises to you so that you're in a state of "wanting nothing," but patience also makes you "perfect," too, which means complete—of full age or mature.

Maturity is part of the process of life. It's part of your destiny to grow and mature, to not only do great things but to become better along the way. A person who is filled with more of the fruit of God's Spirit is a person with the mark of spiritual maturity. Put that in your mental map. Determine in your mind that you are not just mapping toward an external destination, but you are also mapping toward an inner destination—that you are destined to become a person who is more filled with the fruit of God's Spirit.

> But the fruit of the Spirit is love, joy, peace, longsuf-
> fering, gentleness, goodness, faith,
> Meekness, temperance: against such there is no law.

*And they that are Christ's have crucified the flesh with
the affections and lusts.
If we live in the Spirit, let us also walk in the Spirit.*
GALATIANS 5:22–25

Some of these traits of the Spirit are easier than others. For most people, patience (or longsuffering) isn't one of them and temperance isn't either! But it's important to realize that God wants you to become more like Him in patience and in temperament. I know it's not easy, but, with God, it is possible! You can put your flesh down and walk in the Spirit.

If you've got a bad temper, consider it *proving* yourself to God when you choose to be temperate in a situation that would normally set you off.

If you're the most impatient person you know, consider it *proving* yourself to God when you allow the fruit of His Spirit, longsuffering, to flow through you.

As people say, you find out what you're made of when you're under pressure. Try to start seeing those times as opportunities to be more like Jesus. Yes, it's easier said than done, but it is doable.

Do you want to be a success in God's eyes? Then be who He created you to be. Think higher. Do more. But, most important, determine that you're going to be better along the way. Nothing is worth doing or having if you're not stretching yourself to become better in the process.

PAIN IS INEVITABLE, BUT MISERY IS OPTIONAL

In life, pain is inevitable, but misery is optional. Things are going to happen in life. Just because you say the sinner's prayer and accept Jesus into your life doesn't mean that you're going to suddenly avoid all trouble in life. You'll lessen it, but you are not going to avoid all pain no matter what you do.

If you're breathing, you're living in this world, and that means, from time to time, bad things are going to happen. It's just a fact of life. But it is how you go through those situations that matters. I have chosen not to be miserable. There is no reason to be. I don't care what happens to bring my heart pain; God can help me out of it. I can choose to dwell on the bad and remain in misery or look to Him and move through the situation in peace and in joy.

I've tried misery and I don't want it. I've tried sick and broke—and I don't want any more of that either! Sure, pain may come, but I choose how I handle it.

You see, I've determined that, if I can, I am going to take the peaceful path toward my destiny. Sometimes I have to confront situations with the devil and with people but, in the end, I am pursuing my own peace of mind.

I pursue peace when I resist the devil. To give in to him would cause repercussions of misery in my life and in the life of others who follow my ministry.

I pursue peace when I stand up for what's right among others. To not stand up for what's right would cause repercussions of misery for both them and me.

Doing the right thing is always right, but it's not always comfortable. In the end, it *will* bring you peace of mind.

MARRIAGE MAY BE INEVITABLE, BUT MISERY IS OPTIONAL!

Pursuing your destiny will likely include your spouse, if you're married. And, let's face it, there are days when being married isn't easy . . . it's downright aggravating! If you're married, you know what I'm talking about! You can love each other more than anything in the world, but there are days . . . well, you just wish that God would look the other way. Days when you look over at your spouse and wonder who in the world that is?!

Sure, I love my wife, but sometimes, I want to tell her to go home . . . and that ain't to my house! You know what I'm talking about! But you know, even in the hard times of marriage, I've decided that I don't have to be miserable. The same is true for you.

After all, if you are linked up with another person in marriage, you're going to need that other person to accomplish what is in your heart—end of statement. If you consider yourself linked up in the vision, then you have to include your spouse in your vision and that means you have to determine right now that misery is optional. Bottom line? You can't accomplish as much when you are miserable.

You can build a mental map to a good marriage relationship. It starts with being determined not to let the little things of life throw you too far off course in your relationship. Yes, aggravating things happen. Yes, that person can make you angrier than anybody else. But, do you love that person? Did you commit to that person? Then why be miserable? Why focus only on the aggravating things?

Pain is inevitable, but misery is always optional. You choose whether you're going to snap at your spouse. You choose whether you're going to stew in anger. You choose whether you're going to remain in pride and unforgiveness, or whether you're going to take a deep breath, sigh, and try to get to a place of peace. Sometimes you're just going to have to ask for forgiveness, just for the sake of peace. Sometimes you're going to have to sow mercy, instead of doing what you want to do, which may be wrath! You know it's true!

Look, if you are hooked up in marriage, your destiny should include your spouse. You can't live only for yourself and your own ambitions, and expect to have marital success. Both of you need to know the goal. Both of you need to know where you're headed, and that it's a place you're headed to as a couple, together, no matter what. That's commitment. That's dedication. That's a determined mindset, a mental map.

PRIDE—A RELATIONSHIP KILLER

One of the biggest marriage killers is pride. Pride will lead you on a "gloom-despair-and-agony-on-me" path. I'm not talking about the good kind of pride, which is self-respect and confidence in yourself. I'm talking about the kind of pride that refuses to compromise and work things out—the "I'm right, you're wrong, end of story" kind of thinking that is on the express lane to misery. Its root is selfishness.

When I was a young man, I didn't understand any of this and it took me many years to understand that "being the man" doesn't always mean I have to enforce my way. Today, I can say that I've lived a little and I've noticed that I like peace better than aggravation. I know that sounds simple, but it is true. I'd rather take the path of peace with my wife, well, at least most of the time! Some things are worth a spat, but not too many.

Most of the time, I decide to just say, "Forget this pride!" Sure, I may think I'm right, but I'm not going to argue with the woman all night long. I've made up my mind, I married this woman and she married me—we said "till death do us part" and there are days that it looks like that vow may happen sooner than expected. That's just a joke, but you get the point!

My wife, Cathy, and I know that the stability of our marriage isn't based on an argument—it's based on our vows of commitment to one another, through thick and thin. So, it doesn't make a marital difference whether we tick each other off one day or not. It doesn't really make a marital difference whether she's right and I'm wrong or vice versa—the marriage still holds. The commitment still holds.

I love her, she loves me, and we recognize that, sometimes, marriage can be a pain in the neck! We're two people with lots of ideas, opinions, and thoughts about how to talk and live. But we know that no matter our differences, pain is inevitable, but misery is optional!

NEVER GIVE PLACE TO THE DEVIL

One way to be sure that the pain of conflict doesn't last too long is to simply obey the Word of God. Ephesians 4:26–27 says, *"Be ye angry, and sin not: let not the sun go down upon your wrath: Neither give place to the devil."* This means that you should never let your anger and aggravation drag out longer than it needs to. You should be able to count the anger in terms of minutes or hours, not days.

Avoid misery and release the anger before you go to sleep. Recognize it as God's way of telling you, "Hey, misery is optional!" Don't give the devil a place in your marriage by continuing to fight into the night—even if you want to!

Yes, you can be angry. You've probably got a right to be. Just don't sin. Consider this: if you go to sleep angry at your spouse, you're in direct disobedience to the Word of God. That's the path to misery.

God knows that you need peaceful rest and you're not going to get it by going to sleep breathing fire and brimstone. You're not going to get it by looking at your spouse across the sheets with eyes that could kill. You're also not going to get it by blocking out the argument and acting as if it never happened.

Be honest, apologize, and let the anger go. Remember, love is not a feeling. It is a commitment.

PASSING IT ON TO YOUR CHILDREN

You can pass on this concept to your children. They see how you act. They hear what you say. They need to see that you are determined in your thoughts to have a good marriage, and to just plain have a good day. They need to see that, if an aggravating thing pops up, you don't follow it to the very end. They need to see that you value love, that you know it's a commitment to love, even when the one you're with is acting unlovable. Your kids need to see you stop and get refocused on the peaceful path. That is going to help them.

They may see you fight, but do they see you make amends? They may hear you say things you wish you wouldn't have said, but do they see you apologize for it? Kids learn from watching. Let them see practically that you have a determined mindset—a mental map—that you are letting lead you to peace. Each day, including today, doesn't have to end in misery, no matter how crazy it started out!

One of the ways you can build a mental map to being a better parent is to take control over what you think about your own children. Sometimes I see parents who do not have good thoughts toward their own kids. I know this because it shows up in what they say. They only pick out their kids' flaws. They only see the bad thing they're doing. There isn't much praise.

If you've fallen into this habit, remind yourself that everybody in this world has flaws. Nobody is perfect. Not your kids . . . and not you. Ease up on the negative mindset. Even if it comes out because you just want them to be better, always nagging at what's wrong isn't helping anything. Determine that you're going to build positive mental maps in your mind that are going to spill out of your mouth.

Tell your kids what they *can* do in life, not what they can't do. Focus on their strengths. Tell them their strengths. Even if they know it already, you're showing them that you see what they're good at. If you see that something makes them feel passionate, praise it. Even if it isn't what you'd like or what you'd do, say something good about it anyway. Never forget what it was like to be really young.

Above all, don't teach your kids to doubt. Doubt is a disease. It just spreads and spreads and ruins a person's passion and faith, and we all need passion and faith to do anything in life.

When I was a child, I always heard my mama say, "That Jesse, I don't have to worry about him, he's going to take care of himself." My mama was reinforcing my take-charge attitude, even as a child. She didn't always say things that were good, don't misunderstand me! But she did notice and appreciate that I was a go-getter from a very young age.

Don't say what you *don't* want to come to pass. Don't bring up what you don't want your kids to do. In other words, saying "You're bad! You never listen!" is reinforcing rebellion in a kid and gives that kid no hope. Instead, spin it positive if you can and say something like, "You're strong-willed, but you're a good kid. You need to listen to what I'm saying so you can be even better." A strong-willed kid may be a great leader one day. Don't kill his desire to lead by labeling him "bad." Redirect him.

. . .

People forget that God made us to rule. Dominion was one of the first gifts He ever gave man in the Garden of Eden. The principle is that we were not created to be ruled over by other people, but to be rulers in our own lives. So, what some people call rebellion in children is really just the God-given, natural desire to lead . . . which is a good thing being used in a not-so-good way.

The goal should be to redirect leadership in positive ways, to give authority in other situations. Nobody wants to be controlled, and that starts at one year of age! We help our kids by steering them in the right direction and pulling them back when they're headed for disaster, but ultimately by guiding them with our authority . . . not our control.

I have one daughter, Jodi, and I always wanted her to have her own spirituality. I didn't want her to serve God because *I* served God, but because *she* wanted to serve God . . . because she knew that it was the best path for living. I gave Jodi a lot of freedom and she made mistakes I wished she wouldn't have, but I figured she wasn't nearly as bad as I was when I was her age, so I cut her some slack!

Cathy did most of the disciplining since I was traveling a lot. She said I made her the "heavy," which I know wasn't good. But there is one thing Jodi always knew about me. I loved her, and I had her back. I told her, "You're my kid and I'll back you. Just don't lie to me and I'll go to bat for you. But if you lie to me, it's going to be ten times worse for you at the house. So, listen to your mama! We'll have a lot less trouble in this house!" I always say I was the head of my house, but that didn't mean I was the boss! Women are running the world!

If you get anything from this portion of the book, get this: Don't say negative things about your kids, in front of them or behind their backs. If you have a kid who is sometimes afraid of heights, don't reinforce that by saying it all the time. If you have a kid who isn't so great at sports, don't reinforce it by saying it. Your kids do not need to hear you, their parent, drag them down. That won't help them at all.

When you're building a mental map to a better family, you have to remind yourself over and over that you have good kids—this is something that you have to establish in your own mind. Your kids aren't perfect. They mess up. So what? Who hasn't? Your kids are yours and, if you want to see them succeed in life, you have to foster confidence in them. You have to foster faith.

Of course, you need to be strong and teach them right from wrong, that's a moot point. But, you also want to reel in your own negative thoughts and negative words so that you don't dump something on them that they simply don't need.

Say what you want. Tell them that they can do anything in life. Sow faith in them concerning God and themselves. Remember, nobody is hopeless no matter how many mistakes he's made. Use your power of influence to lift your kids up, not tear them down. This isn't easy. You may want to lash out when you get aggravated with them, but remember . . . say what you want. Think and speak the end result into manifestation. They will make their own choices when they are older, but at least they'll know that you always had confidence in them. Just knowing that will help them as they make their way through life.

Like you, they are going to go out into the world and will deal with all sorts of situations. They need to know that somebody believes in them and knows that they have what it takes to live a good life and succeed, no matter what they set their hand to do.

CHAPTER 9

IF YOU THINK IT'S HARD, IT WILL BE

THERE ARE MANY things that can plague a mind, and one of them is worry.

Worry is a mental map hijacker. It makes everything harder than it needs to be and it puts stress on you that you just don't need. It's going to take a lot of energy to do what God's called you to do in this life. Why make it harder by adding worry?

If you always worry about your marriage, you're not helping the relationship. If you always worry about your kids, you're not helping them either. Worry is something that robs your thought-life. It steals your focus away from what is good and draws it into the realm of fear. **Worrying will hijack your mental map, if you let it.** So, don't let it!

There's no reason to live with chronic worrying. The Word of God is powerful and it brings peace of mind. But we have to sow it into our heart by spending time reading it and letting its truths sink in. Just like you can't expect to have peace if you never read the Word, you can't expect to live worry-free if you don't take the time to pray and turn your troubles over to the Lord.

God will take it from you, but you've got to give it and you can't give something to God if you're not in His presence. The Bible says that God is a Spirit, so you have to communicate with Him through your own spirit, and you do that when you pray and open yourself to Him.

"God is a Spirit: and they that worship Him must worship Him in spirit and in truth" (John 4:24).

I don't worry. I used to, but I don't anymore. Why? Because I know I don't have to. I *know* that God loves me. I know it through and through. I know He's with me, no matter what.

Worrying brings more problems into life. If you want to get rid of it, you've got to make a choice to dive more into the Word of God in your private time because Romans 10:17 says, *"So then faith cometh by hearing, and hearing by the word of God."* You've also got to pray.

When you pray, start by worshiping God. This is a state of opening yourself up to God and recognizing His greatness. Tell God how much you appreciate Him. Tell Him what you are thankful for. Start to dwell on the "bigness" of your God. Whatever comes to your mind, just let it out in worship to Him. That frame of mind and openness of spirit will pop open your ability to receive and to release. You'll gain peace and you'll be able to let go of what's worrying you.

You can't talk yourself out of worry, but you can pray yourself out of it. Remember that.

Also, the more you start to see God for what He really is—which is love—the more you will be able to release the habit of worrying.

> There is no fear in love; but perfect love casteth out fear: because fear hath torment. He that feareth is not made perfect in love.
> We love Him, because He first loved us.
> *1 JOHN 4:18–19*

The only reason you can love at all is that you have been made in God's image. So realize the love you have for others is based in God.

Then, realize that if you can love others, how much more can God love you? His love is beyond measuring. And if He loves you that much, don't you think He can help you out in life? Don't you think He can ease your mind and work out the situations that are bothering you?

Don't let worry rob you of peace. God's love casts out ALL fear, and it is necessary for succeeding in life. After all, if your mind is bogged down, how can you think straight enough to build a mental map and run toward your destiny?

HE'S THE PRINCE OF PEACE, NOT THE DUKE OF DOUBT

When you trust Him and put your faith in Him, His peace comes in to help you to set aside worrying thoughts so that you can continue thinking with determination and focus and do what you want to do in life.

To me, peace means possession of adequate resources—nothing missing, nothing broken. God has left us adequate resources, and He's told us to possess them! I don't know about you, but I'm not letting a lying devil from Hell tell me what I can and can't have or do in this life.

Jesus came to give me life and that more abundantly. He said I would do great works, so I will! He said He would never leave me or forsake me, and I believe it! So, I'm never by myself. God is behind me! And if I've got God behind me, then I don't care who is in front of me!

I'm a *Star Trek* fan, and in the television show, they had something they called a "Kobiashi Maroo," which is a term that basically means "a no-win scenario." That's what I tell the devil he's got when it comes to me! I've read the back of the book! He's the loser. I'm moving forward with God and fulfilling my divine destiny.

If the devil gets a punch in now and again, I'm still going to fight the good fight of faith. I win. I'm going to Heaven—it's my destiny. The devil is destined for a lake of fire. That puts things in perspective, doesn't it? I keep my mind-set right, and it keeps me in peace, no matter what is going on.

IF OTHERS CAN DO IT, WHY NOT YOU?

You've heard it said before. The battlefield is the mind. So, make it easy for yourself and decide right now that you're not going to fill your mind with thoughts that will only make life harder for you. This is an effort, but it is worth it. One of the most practical things you can do to start moving forward mentally, is to stop *thinking* that what you want to do is overly hard.

To achieve the results of your mental map, you're going to have to take action on a daily basis. If your mind is muddied up with "can't" and "it's so hard," it will be really hard for you to just do what you have to do each day.

Your mind may want to convince you that fulfilling your destiny, doing whatever God called you to do, is some super-difficult accomplishment. Don't let your mind run wild with "I can't" thoughts. No, it's not easy, but it is doable. If others have done it, why can't you? If God has put it on your heart, why not go for it?

Is it an effort to stop letting your thoughts run wild into negativity? Yeah, it's not easy to reel in your thoughts. If you struggle in this area, it's because your mind has been conditioned to accept negativity as being "real" or rational.

The easiest thing to do in life is nothing. If you want nothing, think that way. Do nothing and you'll get nothing. But if you want to go somewhere in your life—with your marriage, with your kids, at your job, with a dream, or whatever—then you have to win the battle in your own mind.

Remember, you have to win in your mind before you can win in life. When you commit your mind to trusting in God and in yourself, you may have to pray about it every morning. If you are prone to thinking negatively, consider every morning an opportunity to remind yourself, "Christ is in me and I'm in Him. I can do this because I'm

not alone, He's guiding me, and nothing is impossible with Him."
Pray over yourself.

Now, the flip side is obvious. If you want to make anything harder
than it is, all you have to do is start *thinking* about how hard it is and
telling yourself things like, "What am I thinking? I can't do this? I
can't do anything." If you let your mind take over like that, you won't
want to get out of bed in the morning. You'll dread the day. You'll be
so locked up mentally that you'll barely be able to do anything for
God or for others.

Turn your thoughts around. When you have doubts, doubt your
doubts. Instead of letting "I can't" run through your mind, make a
decision to lean on the Word of God and quote it to yourself by saying, "I can do all things through Christ who strengthens me!" (Philippians 4:13, NKJV).

Remind yourself of who you are in Christ Jesus. Condition yourself by speaking good. Remind yourself that living for God is a better
lifestyle—it's how you were created to live. You see, you have to condition your mind to think higher. That doesn't happen overnight, but
it can happen night after night. The Word builds faith and confidence
accrues confidence. The more of God's Word you put in, the more
faith comes out, which gives you confidence.

You see, there is peace in taking it one day at a time, which is
why Jesus told us not to worry about tomorrow. This passage below
is from the book of Luke, and it illustrates perfectly the type of trust
that Christ wants us to have.

> . . . Therefore I say unto you, Take no thought for your life,
> what ye shall eat; neither for the body, what ye shall put on.
> The life is more than meat, and the body is more than
> raiment.
> Consider the ravens: for they neither sow nor reap;
> which neither have storehouse nor barn; and God feedeth
> them: how much more are ye better than the fowls?

And which of you with taking thought can add to his stature one cubit?

If ye then be not able to do that thing which is least, why take ye thought for the rest?

Consider the lilies how they grow: they toil not, they spin not; and yet I say unto you, that Solomon in all his glory was not arrayed like one of these.

If then God so clothe the grass, which is to day in the field, and to morrow is cast into the oven; how much more will he clothe you, O ye of little faith?

And seek not ye what ye shall eat, or what ye shall drink, neither be ye of doubtful mind.

For all these things do the nations of the world seek after: and your Father knoweth that ye have need of these things.

But rather seek ye the kingdom of God; and all these things shall be added unto you.

Fear not, little flock; for it is your Father's good plea- sure to give you the kingdom.

LUKE 12:22–32

DESTINY, DAY BY DAY

Let's face it, you've only got twenty-four hours in every day, some of which you sleep. God may give you ideas, concepts, and insights that you can get determined to follow. They may be your destiny. But no matter what, your life is going to happen day by day and your destiny will be fulfilled as you are seeking the kingdom of God—which is His way of doing things.

God wants you to go to Him for help situation by situation. He's the One who guides your steps if you are following His ways. You've got to keep Him close and follow His lead, day by day, and not get caught up in the mind-set that just robs you of all your peace. Every day you'll have opportunities to stay focused. Every day you'll have opportunities to put your faith in God. Every day you'll have opportunities to move forward in whatever mental map you've made.

If you mess up today, guess what? Tomorrow cometh! God is still on the throne, waiting to help you and wanting to inspire you through His Word to press on. Every day is an opportunity to start again, to do what God's called you to do and to be the person He's created you to be. That's how you move toward your destiny.

Of course, the more you choose the righteous path, the farther along you'll be. But don't allow the idea of living by faith and acting on the Word to overwhelm you. Refuse the type of thinking that says God's way is too hard for you. It's not!

When you change your perception, you'll notice that it's a lot easier for God to help you out! He doesn't have to fight your mind so much! So, life changes will be a lot easier for you. It's not hard to live debt-free. It's not hard to live healed. It's not hard to fulfill your destiny as a joyful, peaceful, patient, successful, and strong person of faith.

Read the Word and let it stir your faith in the areas you struggle with. Let the Word start renewing your mind in these areas so that you can see that it's not only possible, it's inevitable! God's Word **will** work.

What you want is to possess the promise, and that takes action on your part! Think right. Build your mental map. Act on the Word. If you do, you'll receive what God has for you sooner. Remember, it's *not* hard to believe!

EVEN WEIGHT LOSS STARTS IN THE MIND

God can help you accomplish anything, even weight loss. Build a mental map and go toward your divine destiny. This is an area that many believers struggle with, and guess what? It's *not* our destiny!

Now, I could care less if someone is fat or skinny, that's up to them. I can't stand condemnation! Don't let anybody tell you how you should look. You're YOU, and it's nobody's business if you're fat, skinny, tall, or short. God loves you and, if you love you, who cares what "they" think?

But if you need to be healthier and weight is holding you back, don't be a slave to it another day. Start changing the way you *think* about it. Build a mental map by getting determined in your thoughts that you—the real you—is healthy, whole, and fit. Start seeing yourself healthier in your own mind. Reconditioning your mind to stop seeing yourself as defeated, unable, or unfit is the first step to actually doing what's right physically.

Determine to build a mental map and digest it, so to speak, every day. Let that image that you create in your mind of a healthy "you"— spirit, soul, and body—drop from your mind into your heart. How do you do that? Confession.

CONFESSION—A BIBLICAL PRINCIPLE

Confession is a word that a lot of Christians don't like. They think of "name it and claim it" theology as some wacky idea, but the bottom line is that confession is God-driven. Romans 4:17–18 shows us that even God believes in confession as a method of bringing faith-concepts into reality. Abraham followed in God's ways by also believing in confession. *"(As it is written, I have made thee a father of many nations,) before him whom he believed, even God, who quickeneth the dead, and calleth those things which be not as though they were. Who against hope believed in hope, that he might become the father of many nations; according to that which was spoken, So shall thy seed be."*

So, confession is a real and solid biblical principle. If you say something enough to yourself, you will start drawing it into your reality. That is the bottom line. It is a spiritual truth. God said let there be light, and there was light. Abraham said, I'll be the father of many nations, and he became the father of many nations. What are you saying?

If you say that you can't, you can't. You are actually using faith, but you are drawing yourself in the wrong direction, in a direction you don't want to go. So, ask yourself, where do I want to go? What do I want to do? This can apply to anything—your vision to reach people for Christ, your business, your family, whatever. Focus your thoughts by mental mapping, and then confess what you want. Speak it into reality. I know this sounds heady and lofty. It may sound crazy. That's all right.

Remind yourself that 1 Corinthians 2:14–16 says, *"But the natural man receiveth not the things of the Spirit of God: for they are foolishness unto him: neither can he know them, because they are spiritually discerned. But he that is spiritual judgeth all things, yet he himself is judged of no man. For who hath known the mind of the Lord, that he may instruct him? But we have the mind of Christ."*

The natural mind doesn't understand faith. It doesn't understand confession. That's why you have to accept it as a spiritual concept that works, regardless of what your natural thinking tells you. Just do it. Just believe it.

THINK AND CONFESS YOUR BODY INTO SUBJECTION

When it comes to your body and your weight, stop telling yourself how hard it is to lose weight—because it isn't that hard. You can do it. Your body will listen to your mind, and it will do what you tell it to do. But if you don't reel in your "can't" thoughts, your body will control your life.

If you don't *say* what you want, you won't *have* what you want. Speak to your body. Tell it that it will be fit and healthy. Call yourself strong. Do what Joel 3:10 says, *". . . let the weak say, I am strong."*

The weak must say—they must speak—strength. Do that with your physical body.

I find that most people focus on the food part so much when, in reality, it is the mind that needs the most reconditioning. The body is a follower. The mind wants to rule. That's natural. But God wants us to supersede natural thinking by letting our spirit-man rule. Our spirit is reconditioned by the Word of God, which always tells us that we can do anything with God's help and always tells us how to be free. Start telling yourself that you are free and, in time, you will be.

Nobody can stick to a new habit without keeping his mind in the right place, and God can help you with that. Just like you have to stir up the gift of God in you when it comes to spiritual things, you'll also have to stir up the gift of God within you when it comes to physical things.

If you'll get rid of the thinking that says *I can't* and *I never will* and start realizing that you *can* do it because God is with you, that it isn't *that* hard because God is helping you, then you'll start saying it . . . and then you will start doing it. That's when you'll start succeeding.

Don't get ahead of yourself and just plow into doing. Do the steps. Think right. Talk right. Then you'll have success in doing right. No, you may not do the right thing all the time, but you'll be on the road to your divine destiny as a healthier person.

Words matter. What you say about yourself to yourself is going to determine whether you stay on the road to your divine destiny or sit along the sidelines watching others go by. Remember, you are more than a conqueror! If God is for you, who or what can be against you? You can think, you can say, and you can do ALL things through Christ who strengthens you!

Here's a Scripture that I like: *"But [like a boxer] I buffet my body [handle it roughly, discipline it by hardships] and subdue it, for fear that after proclaiming to others the Gospel and things pertaining to it, I myself should become unfit [not stand the test, be unapproved and rejected as a counterfeit]"* (1 Corinthians 9:27, AMP).

This is, of course, talking about keeping your spiritual life straight, but there is also a lesson in here about staying on course physically. Nothing comes without a price. Even salvation came at a great cost to Christ. Buffeting your mind is crucial to being successful spiritually, physically, and even financially.

Thinking, saying, and doing right when it comes to your physical body is a situation-by-situation thing, and you'll have an opportunity to choose today. Like anything else, successful weight loss starts in the mind! Build your mental map and follow through with confession and action, and you're going to see a fit body in the mirror one day soon.

YOUR EFFORT WILL PAY OFF

What kind of effort is required of you to achieve what you want? What's it going to take? You know the answer. It takes everything you've got. Everything is connected. You can't build a house without a foundation. Your thoughts are your foundation—like a concrete slab that you build your house upon. Your action is like the walls going up—wood studs that hold drywall, electricity, and plumbing. Every step you take in building a house is needed to make the house solid.

Any effort that you make toward your goal, toward what is in your mental map, is worth taking. It may not be the roof, but it may be a wall! It may not be the electrical, but it may be the plumbing! What you think is connected to what you do, and what you do is connected to what you'll have and what you'll become in the process. Your destiny comes in baby steps some days; it comes in giant steps other days. The important point is to see that your efforts are the actions that build on your mental map, and they are worth it!

For every action you take, there will be a reaction. It's cause and effect at work. One action leads to another, which leads to another. The point is to get up in the morning and make another step. Don't worry if it seems like the goal is far off. Every step you make will draw you closer to your goal, closer to seeing your mental map become a reality!

CHAPTER 10

SACRIFICE—THE SUCCESS-PRODUCING QUALITY OF A DOER

NOT LONG AGO, I turned on my television and saw that they were broadcasting one of the Triple Crown horse races called the Preakness. I don't remember the name of the horse that won, but I did notice that during the race, he stumbled. Now, in most horse races, a stumble means a loss and possibly even death for the jockey. But in this case, the will of both the horse and the jockey sustained them. Although they almost went down, the funny thing is . . . it didn't stop them from winning. It took double the effort, but the horse and jockey both recovered from the stumble and went on to win the race!

In this race of life, it may take you double the effort to reach your destiny, but you will get there if you do one thing—get back up and keep running! A stumble is not a loss. It's just another opportunity to get back up and succeed. Spiritually, physically, and financially, you are destined to overcome!

You will have many opportunities to trust God and many opportunities to doubt. If you stumble in your faith, don't let it stop you from running your race. Like the winning horse and jockey, you can be the one that pulls out all the stops. You can be the one that gets back up and runs the race until he wins!

SOMEBODY IS GOING TO SUCCEED, WHY NOT YOU?

The bottom line is that somebody is going to succeed. Somebody's going to win. Why can't it be you?

Most people who have seen great success with God have not been perfect, but they've been faithful. They are the types of believers who don't give up. That jockey and horse won a great prize that day, but it took an overflow of tenacity and strength to do it. It took sacrifice. You see, diligence to get back up will help you to regain ground if you stumble.

I believe that God wants the body of Christ to overflow with goodness—with love, with joy, with peace, with prosperity, with health, and with good relationships. When I see people pushing themselves to go the distance, receiving their healing and having financial breakthroughs, I see overflow! An overflow of will, wisdom, faith, good thoughts, and good actions. Some may stumble along the way, but those who don't give up and continue to move forward in faith are the ones who receive the promises of God.

Is it a sacrifice to get back up? Yes. It takes effort and will to get back up after you've struggled or even fallen. Is it worth it? Yes! Success is most definitely worth the sacrifice.

GOD TAKES PLEASURE IN YOUR SUCCESS

God loves you. There's no doubt about it. Throughout His Word, He gives you verse after verse about His unconditional love toward you. Why? Because He is trying to build a mental map in your head about how much He loves you! This world will cut you down. The devil and even your own thoughts will try and tell you that you're nothing, that you aren't valuable and aren't worth the effort. Those thoughts are lies from the pit!

God loves you no matter what you look like, what you say, or even what you do. His love never fails. But that's no excuse to live beneath your benefits. God's Word will show you how to live the good life, a life of success, spiritually, physically, and financially. Of course, it begins with salvation, but that is not the end. It's the start of a new life with new ways of living that can help you to overflow in the God-kind of life that brings real success.

You see, you've got to get it in your mind that God *wants* to see you succeed. He is not against you; He's for you. He's not looking to take from you; He's looking to give to you. The Word says it gives God great pleasure to see you prosper.

Psalm 35:27 says, *"Let them shout for joy, and be glad, that favour My righteous cause: yea, let them say continually, Let the LORD be magnified, which hath pleasure in the prosperity of His servant."*

It actually brings God pleasure when you enjoy the fruit of your labor and the harvest of your sown seeds. It magnifies Him. He wants to see you shout for joy and be glad. He wants to see you favor His righteous cause, or in other words, do the right thing in life.

SUCCESSFUL THINKING, SUCCESSFUL DOING

Success with God is determined by adherence to His Word and His cause. That means that you need to move beyond determined thoughts, and into determined actions—moving forward by doing the right thing, situation by situation, whether it's comfortable or not.

It may be comfortable to dream. It may be comfortable to create determined thoughts, to come up with ideas, to share those ideas with others. It may be uncomfortable to take the next step and actually do something about what you want.

Doing is sacrificial by nature. This is true with anything you set your hand to do. It is a sacrifice to actually do what it takes to create peace in your marriage. It is a sacrifice to do what it takes to lead your kids in the right direction. It is a sacrifice to build your business, or to take your business to the next level. It all requires you to break out of your comfort zone, and sacrifice the lifestyle that you have right now.

Sacrifice is in every success. Consider living for God. When you are merciful to somebody, when what you really want to do is show him some of your wrath, you're sacrificing your own wants for God's wants—and that leads to godly success.

When you choose to show dignity and respect for someone or something when it's easier to be one of the disrespecting crowd, you're sacrificing your own wants for God's wants—and that leads to godly success.

It comes down to what you believe and what are you willing to *do* about it. Are you willing to sacrifice your preconceived ideas about yourself? Are you willing to sacrifice the lusts of the flesh for the fruit of the Spirit?

THE QUALITIES OF A DOER

Look around you at the successful people that you know or admire. Did they achieve their success easily? Probably not. Real success requires that you sacrifice something of yourself, whether it's time, money, your fleshly tendencies, or whatever. Something must be sown for something to be reaped.

A doer is someone who isn't afraid to make the sacrifices necessary to see his or her heart's desire become a reality. A doer is someone who moves beyond mental mapping, beyond ideas, and into action. Here are some qualities of a doer:

1. Doers are not lazy.
2. Doers are willing to work in whatever circumstances are necessary.
3. Doers are willing to change and exchange old methods for new methods.
4. Doers are proud of what they've done, but they aren't satisfied with stopping.
5. Doers *do!*

Doers make the world go around. We write about them. We talk about them. We are amazed by their focus, their tenacity, and their accomplishments. What do they have that non-doers don't have? Determination. They bring mental mapping—determined think-ing—into determined doing!

Just as determined thinkers do not just let their thoughts run wild just to see where the thoughts may splatter, and just like confessors do not speak just to see where the words may splatter, so doers do not act just to see where their actions may splatter. Doers are focused in what they do and most important, they're willing to make sacrifices in order to reach their goals in life—whether they are spiritual, physical, or financial—and that's what makes them succeed where others fail.

This, of course, pertains to the Word of God, too.

A DOER OBEYS THE LORD

God calls us to not just believe what He says in His Word, but to *do* what He says, too. While believing and speaking out your dream or ideas is crucial, it is action that must come next if you want results. The Bible puts it this way:

> *But be ye doers of the Word, and not hearers only, deceiving your own selves.*
>
> *For if any be a hearer of the Word, and not a doer, he is like unto a man beholding his natural face in a glass:*
>
> *For he beholdeth himself, and goeth his way, and straightway forgetteth what manner of man he was.*
>
> *But whoso looketh into the perfect law of liberty, and continueth therein, he being not a forgetful hearer, but a doer of the work, this man shall be blessed in his deed.*
>
> *JAMES 1:22–25*

A doer doesn't waddle in as much confusion. A doer recognizes the freedom or liberty of living by the Word. A doer is blessed.

A hearer is self-deceived. A hearer goes between clarity and confusion all the time. He's forgetful. What does a hearer forget? He forgets who he is "in Christ."

Like a man looking in a mirror and walking away, forgetting what his face really looks like, a hearer gets revelation knowledge and a clear vision of who he is in Christ. He's on fire for a moment. He's confident. Then he leaves the service or puts down the Word and goes about his day. He doesn't do anything differently, so in a short time he's right back where he started, not knowing who he really is in Christ.

The role of a doer is to walk in obedience—to simply obey God. The real Christian life is not about just talking the talk, but walking the walk. And that is a sacrifice in more than one way. It's sacrificing *our* way for *God's* way, in an effort to walk the *best* way.

SUCCESS AND SACRIFICE

I believe it with everything I am . . . you cannot have success without sacrifice. They work hand in hand. You may ask, "So, what happens if I succeed without sacrificing? Or, what happens if I sacrifice but don't see success?" The answer can be found in a statement I heard a long time ago:

If I succeed without sacrifice, then it is because someone went before me and made that sacrifice. If I sacrifice and don't see success, then someone who follows will reap success from my sacrifice.

Oftentimes, our success is generational. How often in the Word do we read about the "children's children" and about God honoring one person on behalf of another—sometimes their parents and grandparents?

Proverbs 13:22 tells fathers that, *"A good man leaveth an inheritance to his children's children: and the wealth of the sinner is laid up for the just."*

As you grow older, you begin to realize the magnitude of the generational blessings of God. You begin to see that there are some things in your life that you aren't doing for yourself. You're doing it for the next generation, and sacrifice is part of your destiny.

You see, your destiny doesn't end with you. Beyond your occupation, beyond your dreams, you have a spiritual purpose that is meant to be carried on in some way to the next generation. This is why it's so important to pass your knowledge of spiritual things on to your loved ones.

What you leave as an inheritance—spiritually, financially, or in any other way—should flow to your children and your children's children. It should serve as a foundation for them to build upon.

Your kids should know what it means to be saved and secure in the love of God. They should know what it means to pursue righteousness, to receive grace and mercy, and to follow their own destiny, wherever it leads them.

I hear a lot of people say, "Well, the Lord didn't bring this to pass in my life . . ." and I just stop them right then and there. "No," I say, "If you sacrificed, success is coming. You are going to be rewarded, but you also have to realize that you've paved the way for another. God used you as a builder for the next generation, and they will reap from your sacrifice."

The Apostle Paul said that there are some who sow and some who water, but it is God who gives the increase.

I have planted, Apollos watered; but God gave the increase.

So then neither is he that planteth any thing, neither he that watereth; but God that giveth the increase.

Now he that planteth and he that watereth are one: and every man shall receive his own reward according to his own labour.

For we are labourers together with God: ye are God's husbandry, ye are God's building.

*According to the grace of God which is given unto me, as a wise masterbuilder, **I have laid the foundation, and another buildeth thereon.** But let every man take heed how he buildeth thereupon.*

For other foundation can no man lay than that is laid, which is Jesus Christ.

1 CORINTHIANS 3:6–11

A LAYER IN GOD'S PLAN

Christ sacrificed His life on the cross. Was it for Himself? No, it was for us, for future generations. Christ was a layer in God's work—the most important layer, yes, but we reaped the benefits of His great sacrifice.

For years I thought that *everything* I sowed and sacrificed would cause me to automatically reap the benefits for myself, but I've come to realize that there are some things that I have built that are a foundation for the next generation.

I now know that I may have dreams that I put into a mental map. I may be determined in my thoughts, determined in my actions, and make every spiritual and physical stride to accomplish what I know God has put on my heart. But even then, I may not be the one to see my dream come to fruition.

It is very possible that I am a layer in God's plan for the next generation. Even though I obey God and take heed in regard to what I do for Him, I know that, if I don't see success with my own eyes, God will be faithful to my vision and someone else will reap the benefits of all my prayers and all my work.

Now, I do believe in the thirty, sixty, and hundredfold return. I believe in sowing and reaping spiritually, physically, and financially. I've reaped a hundredfold on my giving many, many times, but there are some things that I've done that I now realize are not really for me, but for the next generation.

For example, look at a church in your local community. If it was built strongly, most of the men and women who built that church will not outlive the actual building. They will go by the way of the grave, but the church building will still stand. In other words, those who sacrificed their hard-earned living, their ideas, designs, and time did not receive the full reward of their labor. Instead, they were a "layer" in God's will for that community. They laid a foundation that lasted beyond their own generation.

I believe that every person's work is a continuation of another's. We're connected. Someone will always come along to add to the dream, idea, or concept. Someone will come along and perfect what you've done. Every idea can be perfected and made better. Every dream can continue.

You may be the originator, but you may not receive the accolades. The one who comes along after you and perfects your idea may receive the accolades. Don't let that bother you. Remember, without that originator, there was nothing. Honor will come to you, whether it is through people or simply from your God. He sees. He knows. He's going to honor and reward you for anything good that you bring into this world.

Never forget that statement: If you enjoy success without sacrifice, it's because someone else made the sacrifice for you, and if you sacrifice but don't see the fullness of your success, you can take it to the bank that someone will come behind you—your children and children's children—and reap from your sacrifice. You may be a layer in the vision, but it will come to pass. God is always faithful.

JEWS, GENTILES, AND THE GRAND-CATS

Cathy and I have only one child. She's a grown woman now and married—so at the time of the writing of this book we've got a grand total of four in our family: Cathy and me, our son-in-law, Eddie, and our daughter, Jodi—that's it.

Well, I take that back, we have to count the grand-cats. We've got three of them—Sammy, Minette, and Holiday. We used to have only one grand-cat for fifteen years, Mia, but she bit the dust, and now we've got three new ones.

Two are like the Jews. Sammy and Minette are the chosen ones. Purebred and hand-selected, these cats were bought at a high price! The other is like the Gentiles. She wasn't chosen, and she wasn't hand-selected. This cat just showed up at the Promised Land right next to the Thanksgiving holiday, hence her name. She fell on the mercy of the house and cut the covenant! Now, Holiday has been adopted into the family. You could say that she's chosen. She's royal. She's part of a holy, and most certainly peculiar, people!

God cares about the whole family, even about those members that don't seem like they belong at all! His hand of blessing is extended to your children and your children's children! I told my daughter, "If you don't give me grandkids, those are going to be the richest cats in the city of New Orleans!"

You see, God wants our children and our children's children to inherit His blessings—spiritually, physically, and financially. Your destiny isn't to be sad, sick, broke, and disgusted! It's your destiny to live long and prosper, in every way. It's also your children's destiny to reap the benefits of your sacrifice.

I believe that God's plan is to show you His salvation, to bless the work of your hands, and the land that you own and everything that comes under your care. That includes animals if you have them, crops if you grow them, and businesses if you have them, too! Your family is something that God cares about.

YOU DON'T HAVE TO BE A MONK, JUST LOVE GOD

God tells us to teach our children; to train them in His ways. I believe that all believers should make training your kids in the ways of God a personal goal in life. It's not about making them religious monks—that will only drive them away. This is about giving your kids life skills that are based on God's Word.

Children need to know that living for God is good and right, not weird. This is the way people are supposed to live—moral, good, positive lives. Sin came in and ruined a lot but, through Jesus, we can get back to living good and right.

As believers, we shouldn't train our kids to think we're in some "us" and "not them" club. Salvation is for everybody. I figure that people who don't know God either just haven't heard about Jesus's great sacrifice or just haven't yet realized that it's a good way to live. If you train your kids in the ways of God, they'll have some spiritual skills and, even if they stray, they'll have something to fall back on when they finally get their head straight.

I told my daughter, Jodi, "You don't have to be a monk, just love God." She knew that serving God was her choice, not mine. She knew I couldn't control her and *make* her love God. All I could do was tell her what happened to me and show her ways to live for God that would make her life better. I used everyday life to show her how to live. I wasn't perfect and she saw that, but she also saw that I loved God and wanted to do right. That alone helps kids see that doing right is worth pursuing.

I encourage you to build a mental map on the road to your children's divine destiny by making sure that they have a spiritual foundation. Lay it down strong, because this world is tough. Sugar-coated Christianity is for the birds. Your kids need to know that Jesus is real and that He loves them and wants the best for them always.

GOD SEES THE FUTURE GENERATIONS

Deuteronomy 6:7 says, *"And thou shalt teach them diligently unto thy children, and shalt talk of them when thou sittest in thine house, and when thou walkest by the way, and when thou liest down, and when thou risest up."*

God is interested in the family. He has us covered from A–Z! If the average life span of people today is eighty years, then I believe that every time God looks at us, He looks at least two hundred and forty years into the future—three generations deep!

Why can't you look three generations deep, too? Why not determine in your thought-life and your prayer-life that your children will grow in the ways of God and serve Him all the days of their life? Why not? They have their own free will, of course, but you have the power of influence, the power of prayer, and God can give you wisdom in sharing what you know with your kids.

Throughout the Word of God, we hear promises toward our children's children, which is why I believe that, when God looks at you, He sees your kids and grandkids. And I believe that He wants to provide for you and your family in every way—spiritually, physically, and financially!

Your kids are going to have questions. They're going to look to you as a guide to how to live. Show them the best you can and tell them that you're not perfect, but you serve a perfect God. What you don't understand about God isn't an excuse to cut down God. Never cut down God around your kids, ever. Determine in your mind that God is good and that just because you don't understand something doesn't mean that God has done something wrong. He's never wrong.

If your kids ask questions about God or life that you don't know the answer to, don't make something up just because you want them to see you as strong. You don't have to know it all. Just tell them, "I don't know, but I'm going to try and find out." Then, pray and ask God to lead you to the answers. When your kids see that you seek God and His Word for answers, you're giving them a tool for future use. They will one day follow your example and that will help them to serve God on their own.

God will honor your children. He loves them more than you do. How many times have I read where God said something like, "I remember My servant Abraham" or "I remember My servant David and I will not allow this or that to come upon his children or his seed." Read your Bible and you'll see how amazing and honorable God is!

GOD IS MOVED BY FAITH

God is no respecter of persons (Acts 10:34). What He has done for others, He will do for you. But never forget that God isn't moved by crying and complaining. He's moved by tenacious faith. He isn't moved by need, either. If He was moved by need, He'd never get out of India, where need exists by the truckloads. God shows us through His Word that He is moved by our faith. Our success with God comes according to our faith in His ability to perform His Word.

Psalm 115:16 tells us that God has given this earth to us. It says, *"The heaven, even the heavens, are the LORD's: but the earth hath He given to the children of men."* That means we have the responsibility to care for this earth and those in it. It is man's inhumanity to man that leaves people hungry and destitute, not God. There is enough food on this planet to feed us all. There is also enough work for us all to have something to do. There is enough for all of us. So, never blame God for what man does. That's a slap in the face to the Creator, who made this world and handed it over to the children of men.

Your future generations are coming out of *you*—so, since they are yours, you might as well think highly of them now and start working toward creating a future for them. Start spiritually. Do what Proverbs 22:6 says and, *"Train up a child in the way he should go: and when he is old, he will not depart from it."* This is following through on a mental map that is determined to lay a spiritual foundation for future generations.

I've decided that I am having faith for my future generations . . . even though, lately, it looks like it's just going to be a few cats! But, hey, I'm putting my trust in God! I'm sacrificing and laying a foundation knowing that God will take care of my family. I know, without a shadow of doubt, that He will cause me to reap, generation upon generation! I am doing my part, and I know that God is doing His!

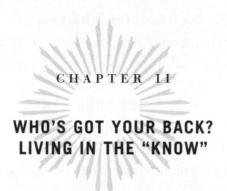

CHAPTER 11

WHO'S GOT YOUR BACK?
LIVING IN THE "KNOW"

I LOVE THE confidence that the Apostle Paul had in Jesus. He said, "... *I **know** whom I have believed, and am **persuaded** that He is able to keep that which I have committed unto Him against that day"* (2 Timothy 1:12). He was persuaded that God was a keeper of His Word. He didn't just believe it, he *knew* it! Do you?

Do you really *know* that God keeps His Word? If you know it, your life will show it. You'll be confident in God. People around you may even think you're a little cocky when it comes to believing the Word. But you'll know that they just don't *know* it like you know it!

You see, when you spend time in the Word and your faith builds, you're going to start seeing yourself more like God sees you. You're going to start formulating your own mental map of faith that you will use to take you where you want to go in life. God's will for your life will actually become your dreams.

When God drops something in your spirit, realize that it's from Him. Digest it. Meditate on it. Make it part and parcel of yourself. When you do that, you begin thinking differently. You find yourself in the "know," fully persuaded that what God said, He will do! And that kind of thinking is what puts you smack dab in the middle of the road that is going to lead you to your divine destiny!

WHO'S GOT YOUR BACK?

Paul the Apostle knew that no situation or person could overpower God Almighty! The devil may have attacked him while he was living out his destiny, but Paul didn't care. This is what he said about it.

> What shall we then say to these things? **If God be for us, who can be against us?**
>
> He that spared not His own Son, but delivered Him up for us all, **how shall He not with Him also freely give us all things?**
>
> Who shall lay any thing to the charge of God's elect? It is God that justifieth.
>
> Who is he that condemneth? It is Christ that died, yea rather, that is risen again, who is even at the right hand of God, who **also maketh intercession for us.**
>
> **Who shall separate us from the love of Christ?** shall tribulation, or distress, or persecution, or famine, or nakedness, or peril, or sword?
>
> As it is written, For thy sake we are killed all the day long; we are accounted as sheep for the slaughter.
>
> Nay, **in all these things we are more than conquerors through Him that loved us.**
>
> For **I am persuaded,** that neither death, nor life, nor angels, nor principalities, nor powers, nor things present, nor things to come,
>
> Nor height, nor depth, nor any other creature, **shall be able to separate us from the love of God, which is in Christ Jesus our Lord.**
>
> ROMANS 8:31–39

Those Scriptures are so deep with revelation that you could take just one verse and spend a lifetime on it. I encourage you to meditate on this passage. Get to *know* that God is for you and, if He's for you, then what can really stand against you? He's got your back!

Knowing that God has got your back, and that *nothing* can separate you from His love, will give you peace and confidence. It will help you to make those sacrifices that you need to make in order to succeed.

Your destiny doesn't end with you. Part of your children's inheritance is the example you leave behind to them. Let your example be full of faith. Let it be full of joy. Let it be full of peace, knowing that God has got your back!

Sacrifice is just part of life. Struggles are, too. But just because obstacles come, doesn't mean you have to cave in. Anxiety hinders success. Fear hinders faith. Yet, God gives you these truths in His Word to help you gain the faith you need to succeed and the peace you need to be able to enjoy your success. Glory!

Besides, if you've got God behind you, then who cares who's in front of you? Problems come, but so what? The devil is a liar, and you can change anything with your faith.

YOU SHALL ARISE!

Anybody can fall down, cry, and quit. Anybody can fear and hide. If you've got God, you don't have to do that. You can lift your head, set your face like flint, and keep the faith. You can speak to whatever problem is rearing its head at you, resist the devil, and get victory.

As God's child, you can go to the throne of grace and get what you need. You can praise God even in the midst of a bad situation. Remember, God can liberate your mind and cause you to see that you will triumph.

Do you remember the story of the stumbling horse from the beginning of chapter ten? That horse could have given up; the jockey could have slowed him down. Neither accepted that stumble as defeat.

No one can keep you down unless you *decide* not to rise again. The only one that keeps you down in life is you, because you have the power of God on your side. The Bible says in the book of Micah, *"when I fall, I shall arise . . ."* (Micah 7:8). I like that! I *shall* arise! There is willpower involved in destiny.

Those who choose to be "more than conquerors," as the Scripture says, may suffer a loss, but they will not be defeated because "a loss" doesn't equal "the end." Tomorrow cometh! You may lose a battle, but you will win the war, because God has written the end of the book!

SUCK IT UP

In my life, I've decided to get up, to suck it up and hold my head high, no matter what. So, I have to sacrifice . . . so what! That's part of living, and I don't mind doing what needs to be done. God will honor me, one way or another. I will see His goodness in my life and my children's children will inherit it as well.

I've had many people lie about me, yet I refuse to get into battle with them. I take my battles to the Lord, to the place of prayer, because that's where I get the strength to continue moving forward.

When struggles come, I could just lie down in the mully-grubs of life and sing the blues all day long. No thanks. Crying and moaning never gets anything done. Though I may fall, I *shall* arise! It's an act of my will and my faith in God.

There were times when I didn't have enough money to eat when I first began preaching the Gospel, but it didn't stop me from doing what God said. I've always been told what I'm *not*. All my life I've heard, "You're not this, you're not that. You ain't this, you're not that. You'll never amount to this; you'll never amount to that." That's how I grew up, always hearing how much of a "nothing" I was.

Today, some people still say the same thing to me. Okay, I understand that they think I'm not much on my own, but with God, I'm *more* than enough! I can say good things about myself because I know that it's not me that liveth, but Christ that liveth in me! Like Galatians 2:20 says, *". . . the life which I now live in the flesh, I live by the faith of the Son of God, Who loved me and gave Himself for me!"* Glory! Let me preach a little!

So, I don't frustrate the grace of God. I decide to stick with God because I know that *"greater is He who is in me, than he that is in the world"* (1 John 4:4). And *"If God be for me, who can be against me?"* (Romans 8:31). I'm more than a conqueror, and if I have faith in God, I can say to that mountain, *"Be thou removed,"* and if I don't doubt in my heart and believe those things that I say, it will come to pass (Mark 11:23).

A delay is not a denial, and every sacrifice I make is a seed for future success! Glory!

SIMPLY BELIEVE, SIMPLY OBEY

You see, I'm *going* to fulfill my divine destiny. I *will* be who God called me to be. I will also *have* whatsoever I say because Jesus said that, whatsoever things I desire when I pray, if I believe that I receive them, then I shall have them (Mark 11:24)!

I know that the Spirit of the Lord God is upon me and He has anointed me to preach this Gospel (Luke 4:18). I have been called to do the works of Christ and greater (John 14:12). The God I serve is able to do exceeding abundantly above ALL that I can possibly ask or think according to the power that worketh in me (Ephesians 3:20). Glory!

Do you see where I'm going with this? Listen, I've filled myself up with the Word and it has set me free—free from the pain of sacrifice, free from the opinions of others, free from the restrictions of what I "can" and "can't" do.

I am moving on the road to my divine destiny. I'm living long and prospering—sticking with Psalm 91:16, *"With long life will I satisfy him, and shew him My salvation."* I simply believe and obey, and He lifts me up!

I challenge you to grab hold of the truths I've shared in this chapter for yourself. Realize that everything you do matters, every sacrifice you make is recorded. Consider them seeds you sow not only for yourself, but for future generations. Meanwhile, God has got your back!

So, get determined in your thought-life. Simply believe God—consider it part of building your mental map. Simply obey—consider it part of being a doer. Remember, if you *only* think, say, and do what you want, the importance of what you do will only last for a season. But, if you think, say, and do what God's Word says, your works will last forever. As Jesus said over and over again, *"Heaven and earth shall pass away, but My Words shall not pass away"* (Matthew 24:35, Mark 13:31).

Forget about what others may say, and concentrate on what God has said. Put your trust in His Word and what He has laid on your heart. It's going to be a daily choice you make, but one that will be the difference between veering off course into confusion and muddy-living, or staying straight on the path that is His will and your divine destiny!

CHAPTER 12

MAKE NO PROVISION FOR FAILURE

I WAS RAISED po'—not poor, po'! What's po'? It's what you are when you don't have enough money for the last two letters!

We had dishes growing up that you could drop on the floor and never break . . . because they were plastic. We had forks that hadn't been straight in twenty-five years. My mama cooked weenie spaghetti and weenie gumbo and weenie whatever else she could scrape up because, most days, sausage was just too expensive. I grew up wearing my brother's outgrown clothes. I grew up not having much of anything and not seeing much of value.

When I was a boy, I did a lot of odd jobs. My daddy started me working eight hours a day at the IGA grocery store when I was eleven. I worked every Saturday for twelve hours and eight hours from Monday through Friday. My dad arranged for the bus to drop me off at the grocery store every day after school at 3 P.M. I worked until 11 P.M. This was before America had child-labor laws, or at least before the bayou country of Louisiana started abiding by them.

I started playing music when I was five years old, and by the time I was a young teenager, I used my talent to play in local bars. I'd sneak out and play until 2 A.M. to make some extra money. No one cared in those days how old you were, as long as you could play, and since I never slept more than five or six hours a night, I could swing the hours. What with work, school, and playing music, the hours weren't easy, but I did it. I felt like I had no other choice.

Throughout my teen years, I was a short-order cook, a soda jerk, a grass cutter, and did just about anything else I could to make a few dollars. When a day job opened that paid higher than the one I had, I switched. Between my day jobs and my late-night music playing, I was knocking down some serious dough! There came a point as a teenager that I was making twice as much as my father, just by the music alone. It became my ticket out of Louisiana and out of poverty.

As a boy, I do remember a few moments where I noticed nice things that others had. Once, I was watching television and saw a woman holding a beautiful china cup. I said, "I'm going to have cups like that one day." My mama said, "Boy, you ain't never going to have anything like that!"

Now, I don't know if she meant to discourage me. It was just the way our family talked. Anything outside of plastic dishes, run-down cars, and weenie spaghetti was for "other people" and not us. I think my mama may have thought she was protecting me from disappointment by telling me not to get my hopes up. I don't know.

When I got older and started earning my own money, I realized that I didn't have to live like my family. I didn't have to think like them. I didn't have to be them. I could make my own way. I realized that, since nobody was going to lift me up, I had to lift myself up. I knew that nobody in my immediate family was going to encourage me, so I had to encourage myself.

I made a decision when I was very young that I wouldn't cut myself down, and I wouldn't make a provision for failure. I knew that my future depended on it. I decided that, if I was going to have or do anything in this life, I was going to have to believe in myself. And whatever I was doing, I was going to have to give it all I had. After all, for me, there was nothing to go back to.

FAILURE IS NOT AN OPTION

There is something to be said for not having anything to go back to. It gives you a different perspective. You know right up front that failure is not an option.

As a born-again believer, I don't have to rely only on myself anymore—thank God! That's too difficult for anyone to do long-term. Yes, I still have to speak good about myself to myself. Yes, I still have to give it all I've got! But I don't have to make it on my own because I have God backing me! I have His Holy Word that I can wield like a sword to cut the devil's plans for my defeat to shreds! Failure is *still* not an option for me.

I want God's best in my life—spiritually, physically, and financially. I don't want to be saved just enough to be miserable. I don't want to live sick when the stripes were laid on Jesus's back for my healing. I don't want to live po' when it is God's favorite wish that I prosper and be in health, even as my soul prospers (3 John 2). Glory! There is a better life for me . . . and there is a better life for you, too!

God has your best interest at heart. If you have eaten on plastic all your life and you want to eat on china, you can do it. If you want to have a relationship that isn't a scream-fest like your parents had, you can have it. If you want to live healthy and whole, not busted and depressed, you can have it.

God wants to birth dreams in your heart. He wants to show you His ways of living, ways that are superior to the ways of the world, ways that don't make a provision for failure!

LOSE THE FAILURE MIND-SET

Failure. Ask yourself how much time you spend thinking about it. You probably think about it more than you realize. Most of us were taught to *not* get our hopes up too high. We were taught to deal with the punches that life throws our way and not expect anything, but this is not the way God wants us to live.

You may have learned to guard your emotions by setting yourself up for failure. That way, if you succeeded you'd be even more thrilled, and if you failed . . . well, you didn't expect it to happen anyway.

Many of us were conditioned to make a provision for failure. If I had a dime for every time somebody told me, "Now, if it doesn't happen, Jesse, you can always . . ." I'd be up to my ears in dimes today! Somebody somewhere always seemed to be giving me a way out "just in case."

In fact, people can make you so jaded about success that you start to think that failure is seeking you out. Have you ever felt that way? Like failure is some kind of predator stalking you, just waiting for the opportune moment to leap out and demolish your plans?

That kind of thinking is diametrically opposed to success. It's the kind of thinking that stops a mental map before it's even formulated. It's why it is so hard for failure-minded people to live the life of faith.

Many of us have been so conditioned to accept failure that the faith-life seems far-fetched. Some of you may think, *How could someone blindly charge forward without making a provision for failure? That isn't too wise! It's downright unrealistic!*

PUT ASIDE "NATURAL" REASONING

To the natural mind, making a provision for failure just makes good sense. You are just being down-to-earth and realistic. But to the Spirit, making a provision for failure is the first step to actually failing. You see, in God's eyes, those "realistic" provisions for failures are simply what He calls a "lack of faith."

The longer I study the Word of God, the more I am convinced of one thing: If you want to walk in the supernatural provision of God and if you want to fulfill your divine destiny, then you must put aside your natural reasoning and make no provision for failure.

"That sounds good in theory, Brother Jesse," someone said, "but I believed God would meet my needs and He didn't do it!" How do I answer that? Well, I answer it with the truth. "Somebody is lying, you or God . . . and I pick you!"

How can I be so blunt about God's provision? Because of Philippians 4:19, *"But my God shall supply all your need according to His riches in glory by Christ Jesus."* And, because the Bible tells me in Numbers 23:19 that *"God is not a man that He should lie; neither the son of man, that He should repent: hath He said, and shall He not do it? or hath He spoken, and shall He not make it good?"* You see, God always does His part. The question is, do we always do ours?

BELIEVING IN GOD AND BELIEVING GOD

You see, there's a vast difference between believing *in* God and believing God. The whole religious world believes in God. But many have a problem believing God, and that is where the answers to all their problems lie.

Think about it. How many Christians do you know who actually believe what Jesus said in John 14:12: *"Verily, verily, I say unto you, He that believeth on Me, the works that I do shall he do also; and greater works than these shall he do; because I go unto My Father."*

Remember, Jesus had strong faith. Jesus resisted temptation and was a man of prayer. Jesus reached out to the lost. Jesus healed the sick, cast out demons, and raised the dead. And that's when He wasn't praying and preaching! That's a tall order, isn't it? Jesus loved children. He was both merciful and just. Although He was a peacemaker, Jesus wasn't afraid to speak up when confronted by the religious men of the day. He hated hypocrisy and went straight to the issues of the heart.

Jesus walked on the water. Jesus turned a two-piece fish dinner into enough to feed five thousand. Jesus spoke to the wind and waves, and they listened. Jesus raised a man from the dead who had been gone for days and stunk! And this is just a fraction of what Jesus did. The Word says, *"And there are also many other things which Jesus did, the which, if they should be written every one, I suppose that even the world itself could not contain the books that should be written. Amen"* (John 21:25).

Now, back to John 14:12 . . . who is it Jesus said would do all this and more? *"Verily, verily, I say unto you,* **He that believeth on Me,** *the works that I do shall he do also; and greater works than these shall he do; because I go unto my Father."*

Do you believe in God or do you *believe* God? The next verse says, *"And whatsoever ye shall ask in My name, that will I do, that the Father may be glorified in the Son. If ye shall ask any thing in My name, I will do it"* (John 14:13–14).

The church world has distorted it. They don't believe that *whatsoever* they ask in His name, He will do. The church believes that Scripture this way: "And *some* things that you ask in My name that will I do." They want to limit God. They're afraid to open that door too wide; they're afraid to use faith.

But do you know what? None of us can get to the level of doing the works of Jesus if we *don't* use faith. If we make provision for failure in our mind, then we are destined to fail. **God** *requires* **us to think higher, to have more faith, if we are to do the works of Jesus— which is part of our divine destiny.** We are supposed to be a people of authority, a people that call upon God in time of need and see results. We are a people of faith! And the more we realize it, the more we use it, the more provision and success we're going to see with God.

THE POWER OF DESPERATION

Don't take my word for it. Look at the Bible and see what God says on the subject. Let's look at the story of Elisha and the widow woman, and see how this can relate to modern life.

> *Now there cried a certain woman of the wives of the sons of the prophets unto Elisha, saying, Thy servant my husband is dead; and thou knowest that thy servant did*

*fear the LORD: and the creditor is come to take unto him
my two sons to be bondmen.*

*And Elisha said unto her, What shall I do for thee? tell
me, what hast thou in the house? And she said, Thine hand-
maid hath not any thing in the house, save a pot of oil.*

*Then he said, Go, borrow thee vessels abroad of all thy
neighbours, even empty vessels; borrow not a few.*

2 KINGS 4:1–3

The first thing I want you to notice is that this lady was very strong in her words to Elisha. She didn't beg him for help. She didn't care if he was busy. She basically said, and I'm paraphrasing, "Look, Elisha, my husband—the guy that used to work for you—is dead. I don't have any money and my creditors are about to take my kids away. What are you going to do about it?"

That's strong. A lot of ministers would say, "What do you want me to do about it? The man is dead and can't work for me anymore. I can't take care of you all the days of my life. I tell you what, we have an account at the florist. We'll send a big array of flowers." In other words, "Be warmed and filled and get out of my face."

But Elisha didn't do that. He'd spent time with Jehovah, and he knew God would back him up. He didn't offer to do just one thing for her either. He didn't even offer to do only two things for her. He said, "What do you want me to do?"

It takes big faith to ask a woman that question. Most women would say, "Sit down and let me tell you!" But before she could answer, Elisha stopped her. Why? He didn't want her to ask for too little. That is God's way. He's into prosperity. He's not a "just enough" God. He's a "more than enough" Provider! Glory!

PREPARE FOR INCREASE

I love what Elisha said next. He said, *"What hast thou in the house?"*

Can you imagine what she must have thought? *If I had anything in my house I wouldn't be standing here telling you I'm about to lose my boys!* "I've got nothing in my house except a little old bottle of oil."

This woman was in need of cold, hard cash and quick. Elisha told her, *"Then he said, Go, borrow thee vessels abroad of all thy neighbours, even empty vessels; borrow not a few"* (2 Kings 4:3).

I believe that was a strong warning Elisha gave her: *"Borrow not a few."* Why did he want her to borrow so many vessels? Because Elisha didn't want her to make any provision for failure.

A lot of people would have stumbled right there. It didn't make a lick of sense to go borrow bottles when the creditors were circling. Most folks wouldn't budge until somebody gave them a logical explanation. In the meantime, they would have missed their miracle.

I've made up my mind that I'm going to be like that widow woman. If God says get ready for the increase, I'll do what He says. I can hear it now, "Yeah, but all you've got is a little!" I don't care about what I've got or what you've got, I'm interested in what God has—and He has a lot! My part is to do what He says. Why is that so hard?

Disobedience always brings failure, but obedience always brings success. Why? Because obedience makes no provision for failure!

CLOSE THE DOOR ON NOSY NEIGHBORS

Let's look at the next instruction Elisha gave the widow woman. *"And when thou art come in, thou shalt shut the door upon thee and upon thy sons, and shalt pour out into all those vessels, and thou shalt set aside that which is full"* (2 Kings 4:4).

Are you wondering why he told her to shut the door before she poured the oil into those vessels? I'll tell you why. Nosy neighbors! People always want to know your business. Elisha told her to shut the door, close the blinds, and don't let people see what she was doing.

You've got to understand this woman ran all over town asking, "Hey, can I borrow your jar? Your bucket? Hold on, I need your thimble, too!"

You know those people were curious! The crowd probably followed her home, but God had already told her to shut the door.

People will destroy the wonderful things God has for you if you let them. If she felt bad about turning them away and let one or two in, she would have missed God's miracle. What did those people have that was so dangerous to the plan of God?

Opinion.

Opinion is nothing more than a transitory form of thought floating on the sea of life that changes with every wave—a lot of words, but true!

God's Word has the final authority, not people's opinions. James 1:5–6 says it plain, *"If any of you lack wisdom, let him ask of God, that giveth to all men liberally, and upbraideth not; and it shall be given him. But let him ask in faith, nothing wavering. For he that wavereth is like a wave of the sea driven with the wind and tossed."*

Wisdom comes from God, but there may be times that He leads you to seek the counsel of anointed people.

NEVER TAKE NO FROM SOMEONE WHO CAN'T SAY YES

Now, I want you to notice something. This woman told her problem to the one person she *knew* could give her an answer—a prophet of God who her husband worked for.

When you hit a wall in going toward your goal and you don't know what to do, you may need to seek counsel or advice from someone that you know can answer you, and God may use that person to help you in a great way, as He did with Elisha and the widow.

Never take no from someone who doesn't have the authority to say yes.

A woman told this to my wife once when we were trying to work out a hotel issue, and I've never forgotten it! There is wisdom in this, so listen up!

That widow could have wasted her breath and her time asking people who didn't have a lick of anointing or sense about what to do in her dire situation. Instead, she sought out the person that had the authority to say yes, so to speak, the one who had the anointing and the power to actually bring some change into her life.

The widow was wise to seek out the prophet. The prophet was obedient to start flowing in the anointing of God. He could have shut that anointing down and sent the widow away. He didn't, and today we have a story that gives us wisdom for life.

OBEDIENCE PRODUCES A MIRACLE

The widow sought wise counsel. She made no provision for failure. Then she obeyed the prophet and did exactly what he told her to do. She borrowed vessels and shut the door on her nosy neighbors.

> So she went from him, and shut the door upon her and upon her sons, who brought the vessels to her; and she poured out.
> And it came to pass, when the vessels were full, that she said unto her son, Bring me yet a vessel. And he said unto her, There is not a vessel more. And the oil stayed.
>
> 2 KINGS 4:5–6

Elisha didn't stick his finger out and miraculously shoot oil out the tip! No, that widow had to work! She had to knock on doors, borrow vessels, and start laying those babies out. What happened as a result of her obedience and her work? Anointing! Power!

That widow woman did exactly what the prophet of God told her to do and her miracle came to pass—the oil stayed! She started pouring that little bottle of oil into those borrowed vessels, and that miracle oil didn't stop flowing . . . until she ran out of jars.

GOD CANNOT GIVE WHAT YOU CANNOT RECEIVE

Now, the question I always had about this biblical miracle is this: How did the oil know when to stop pouring? The oil couldn't see. It couldn't hear the boy say they were out of vessels. God had a lot more oil than what He poured into all those bottles.

Why did it stop?

I believe that it stopped because of a simple spiritual principle I like to call "**God can't give you what you can't receive.**" This principle is why Elisha told the woman to "*. . . borrow not a few.*" In other words, prepare for the increase and don't make any provision for failure!

Did you know that oil could *still* be pouring for that woman and her children's children? God didn't run out of oil; the widow ran out of vessels to hold the oil.

There have been times when I've asked God, "Why didn't You do that for me?"

"I couldn't," He'd answer.

"What do You mean, You couldn't? You're God!"

"You wouldn't let Me."

"How did I stop You?"

"I can't fully bless what I can't fully conquer. I can't fill what I can't have. There are portions of your life that you won't let Me have. Why won't you give them to Me?"

"Because you'd kill it."

"That's right! It's not you that lives, but the Anointed One that lives in you."

You see, the more of myself I give to God, the more dead in Christ I become. **The more I seek to lose my life to God's will, the more I actually gain a life worth living.** That's what Jesus meant in Matthew 16:25 when He said, "*For whosoever will save his life shall lose it: and whosoever will lose his life for my sake shall find it.*"

At the end of the widow woman's miracle, those vessels were full of miracle oil.

Are you full? Do you have so much God in you that it's spilling over onto others? Is the fullness of God pressed down, shaken together, and running over in you? When people get around you do they step into joy? Do they step into peace? Do they see God's hand on your life? Does it show up on your face?

If not, it's time for a funeral. Bury that old man—let God have access into every part of you. He's a giver and He wants to fill you up with good things. Remember, when there is room to receive it, the oil will flow. When you don't give Him any room, no miracle can be done and your destiny can't be achieved. You've got to give God something to work with.

The widow gave her faith. It took a lot of faith to go and borrow those vessels at the word of Elisha, and she did it!

"Then she came and told the man of God. And he said. Go, sell the oil, and pay thy debt, and live thou and thy children of the rest" (2 Kings 4:7).

Elisha didn't just take care of the debt. He knew that just paying off her debts wouldn't solve the problem. The next month she would've been back. "Elisha! Thy servant my husband is dead. Now, I know you paid the light bill last month, but we've got to eat. Those boys eat like horses. What are you going to do?"

Elisha figured the woman would be back every month. So he saved time for everybody by instructing her on what to do with the oil—sell it—which would provide financial freedom for the widow and her sons. That meant she had enough cash to pay all her debts and for retirement! I call that an overflow miracle, but it was conditional upon many things.

Your divine destiny will be conditioned on many things, too. You're going to be challenged. You're going to have some trouble. That is not the issue. It's how you act, who you seek out, and what you do that is going to determine your outcome.

Refuse to be a victim when trouble comes. Act like the widow. Seek out the right people when you need them, and be a doer.

CHAPTER 13

SHUT THE DOOR ON NEGATIVITY

CAN YOU DRAW negativity into your life? Yes, you can. The widow sought out Elisha's positive influence, because she was seeking a positive solution. She did not want her life to end because of poverty.

We are all receptacles. From the time we're born, we're receiving information and being influenced by what is going on around us—by the people around us and the situations we find ourselves in.

Yes, you can build a mental map to misery. It's easy. People do it every day. Just let negativity consume your thoughts, then your words, and it will spill out into your life. You'll draw in exactly what you really don't want. Doubt builds upon doubt. Fear builds upon fear. Worry builds upon worry. They all draw negative things into your mind first, then into your mouth, and then, into your life.

When you determine that you're going to build a mental map toward your divine—which means godly and good—destiny, then you must take steps to eradicate negative influences in your life.

The first step starts with your mind—determining to think God's way instead of this negative world's way. Then it goes into your mouth—speaking God's way instead of this negative world's way.

Then it moves into your life—acting in a way that falls in line with your new thoughts and words. You see, the ball gets rolling and this becomes a lifestyle. Positive builds upon positive, good builds upon good. Do you get the picture?

When you hear someone tell you that you "can't" you have to let what is *in* you—that determination to lead a "can do" life—rise up, and you have to doubt that doubt. You *can*. Period. End of statement.

Don't let the negative influences of others deter you from building a mental map toward your divine destiny. Realize that it's a fact of life that you can be easily "infected" by other people's negativity. You are swimming upstream when you choose a positive, God-filled life. You're the salmon going up the rocks, so to speak! It takes effort, and you can't let others drain you of your choice to live free.

So, you can either get strong enough in your own choice to live a godly and positive life that you can let their negativity roll off of you like water on a duck's back, or you can tell those people that you don't want to hear their negativity anymore and see what happens. Or you can choose to take a break from seeing them for a while. When you're building mental maps, you're working on something . . . and that something is your life, and it's worth swimming upstream for.

MAKE NO PROVISION FOR SICKNESS

My family has been plagued with heart problems for generations. My father had his first heart attack when he was thirty-four. I was about twelve at the time. The doctors came out and said he wouldn't last ten minutes, but God graciously ministered to him.

My oldest brother had his first heart attack when he was thirty-eight. My youngest brother had a quadruple heart bypass when he was thirty-four. At age fifty-one, my Uncle Edward died of a heart attack on a drilling rig out in the Gulf of Mexico.

I am the only man in the Duplantis family who has never had a heart attack. My father, my grandfather, my brothers, and all my uncles had heart attacks before the age of forty. I haven't had any heart trouble whatsoever, and I was born in 1949. You do the math! I've gone way beyond the heart attack age of my family. I believe that it is because of two things: my lifelong commitment to exercise my temple and, most important, my spiritual stance.

You see, when I discovered that Jesus provided healing in the redemptive plan, I made no provision for sickness. I shut the door on heart trouble. I shut the door on cancer. I shut the door on diabetes. I shut the door on hypertension. I chose to make no provision for failure. It was pure survival at work!

Please understand, I don't deny genetics. I don't deny that cancer runs in certain families. I don't deny that heart disease and high blood pressure run in families. I don't deny medical science. I just deny that heart trouble has the right to touch *my* body. I have a destiny to complete, and I refuse to make a provision for failure. I will complete my destiny and reach my destination.

My body is a temple of the Holy Spirit, so I exercise my heart muscle because I know that it is a practical, healthy thing to do. And I exercise my faith by speaking the Word and laying hands on others.

So, when I made it to forty years of age, I shouted! When I made it to fifty, I shouted! Today, I still have no heart problems. I am a walking, talking testimony to faith in God and to building a mental map on the road to divine destiny.

It is my destiny to preach the Gospel and no devil in Hell is going to steal my blood-bought right to health. I refuse to let sickness dictate my future. I will dictate my future by following after God's plan, and His plan is that "by His stripes, ye were healed" (Isiah 53:5).

Like I often say, "were healed" will change "are sick," but you'll have to build that mental map very strongly. You'll have to follow after your faith, not just in your head and not in mere words, but with your whole heart. This can't be something you give only lip-service to—it's got to have heart to work. This is beyond confession, it is possession!

DON'T LET THEM KILL YOU!

I used to preach funerals for my family members, but do you know what started happening? I'd go to a family dinner and hear their warnings.

"Boy, Jesse, you'd better watch out. You're preaching so hard it's gonna hit you before you know it," one would say.

"Bam! A heart attack is gonna get you good," another would say.

"I'll tell you, Jesse, you're going to die." Another would warn, "You'd better slow down."

Over and over, I'd have to endure the same old doubt-filled words, "When it comes, you'll never know what hit you."

Do you know what I finally figured out? They loved me, but they were going to kill me! I loved them, but I wasn't going to let them do it!

Listening to all that talk made provision for failure. It brought sickness right to the forefront of my mind, and it made me have to battle *their* doubts about *my* body.

I decided that I had to do the same thing that widow woman did to her nosy neighbors in order to get her miracle. I had to shut the door. The widow woman shut out her neighbors' opinions. I shut out my family's opinions about my health. If I didn't do it, they would continue speaking death over me which, in turn, would rob me of my divine destiny. It wasn't going to happen! God comes first in my life, not my extended family.

There is a passage in Matthew 12:48–50 that seems very hard on the surface. Jesus was talking to the Pharisees and teaching the people when He got a message that His mother and family wanted Him to stop so they could speak with Him. Jesus said this:

> *But He answered and said unto him that told Him, Who is My mother? and who are My brethren?*
> *And He stretched forth His hand toward His disciples, and said, Behold My mother and My brethren!*

*For whosoever shall do the will of My Father which is in
Heaven, the same is My brother, and sister, and mother.*
MATTHEW 12:48–50

That seems hard on the surface, but in actuality Jesus knew that His family wanted to interrupt His divine destiny. He wouldn't let them do it. He was about His Father's business at twelve years old, and He remained about His Father's business at thirty-one, thirty-two, and thirty-three years old!

When I realized that my well-meaning family didn't get the picture and would continue to speak death over my life, I made my decision to separate myself. I stopped going to certain family members' homes for dinner. It made them mad.

One relative said, "You're cruel!"

"No, I'm not cruel," I said. "You know I'm a nice person."

"Then why won't you come to dinner!"

"I can't. I'm not coming."

Sometimes, I'd be point-blank blunt and tell them that the Scripture speaks against talking death.

"What do you mean?" one of my relatives asked "What scripture speaks against me?"

"Well, it does! It's right here in Proverbs 4:24," I said, *"Put away from thee a froward mouth, and perverse lips put far from thee."*

"Don't get mad at me," I told her. "God said it, I didn't."

You see, they had not allowed the Word of God to penetrate their hearts concerning sickness. All they see is what has happened to the family over the years, and they wanted to impart to me what happened to them. But I refuse to make a provision for failure by listening or agreeing with them.

I'm not saying I'm better than anyone else, but I do believe I can change my life if I walk in the truth of what is written in the Bible. And so can you!

Change your froward mouth and your perverse lips. Close your ears to the opinions of the world and start living without making a provision for failure—even if you have to separate yourself from the doubters.

MAKE NO PROVISION FOR DEFEAT

David faced the same thing when he went to battle against the giant, Goliath. His own brother said, "What are you doing here?" David had to shut the door on his family's perverse words.

Everybody thought he was a kid with nuts for brains. Saul tried to dress David in armor that didn't fit. It's just like religion to try and dress you in something that you don't need. If you're walking in the Spirit, that stuff will never fit. David refused to wear a suit of armor that didn't fit. Goliath was a big boy, dressed in big armor, with a big mouth. David was just a teenager with a slingshot.

As you know from the story, David was so outmatched it looked ridiculous. That is the way our battles are supposed to look. Why? It gives us an opportunity to exercise faith and gives God an opportunity to show Himself strong on our behalf.

David was backed by a big God, and so are we. I'll paraphrase the story from 1 Samuel chapter 17 for this story.

"What are you gonna do?" Goliath taunted. "Throw stones at me? I'm gonna tear your head off and feed your flesh to the birds."

"You uncircumcised Philistine," David answered. Do you know what he was saying? "You fool. You don't even have a covenant with God. I'm a covenant man. You come against me in your strength and your might. I come against you in the name of Jehovah God!"

Goliath did just what the devil does. He screamed, hollered, and threatened the servant of God.

David stood his ground.

My daddy told me years ago, "Son, if you're ever in a fight don't back up. Stand. If you get knocked out, go down from where you were standing. Never back up." David must have heard the same thing. He didn't back up.

Remember that the next time you face off with a giant problem. Don't back down, stand up and hurl your faith in God at the thing!

David whirled that slingshot and flung his stone. Goliath was so protected with armor that no one thought he'd feel that little rock. But God always knows where the enemy is vulnerable.

After David did his part, God took over. He hit Goliath where he was uncovered with a stone—a Cornerstone! An Anointed Stone! *Bam!* That little rock flew right into an unprotected zone right between Goliath's eyes, and the big giant was dead before he knew what hit him.

David still wasn't finished. He took Goliath's sword and cut off his head. Then David took that head—blood and brains flying everywhere—and shook it at the Philistines. They took one look at that scene and ran for their lives.

What made this ruddy-faced boy different from the rest? He made no provision for failure. He didn't have a "just in case" plan. Why? Because he trusted in God—fully—and he wasn't afraid to stand up against a giant of a problem.

WHEN GOD IS POURING OUT, OPEN UP!

Believe God. Trust Him by putting aside your natural thinking, shutting the door to other's opinions, and making no provision for failure.

When God says, "Go get the jars, I'm pouring out My oil of provision," you'd better go get every container you can! Don't just get one or two, because God will only pour out as much as you are able to receive.

When He says, "Go out on the field and sling a stone at that giant in your life," don't shrink back and begin making provisions for failure. Every problem the devil can throw looks insurmountable to the natural eye. It all looks like destiny-killing situations! You might appear to be so outmatched that people begin to laugh at you. When that happens, don't get discouraged.

Hold your head high and remind that ugly giant just who you are in covenant with. Remind that fool that Jehovah God is backing you up. Then pull back that sling and let her rip!

Just like David, God will prove Himself strong on your behalf. And He will even let you cut off the giant's head and shake it in the devil's face! Never forget that God always has the last laugh. *Always!* Just like David, God will honor and elevate you in the sight of others, but only if you trust Him to guide the stone.

Remember, God is on your side. He was with the widow. He was with David, and He will be with you. Whatever your path, whatever your destiny, whatever obstacles you face, God will lead you to victory every time!

CHAPTER 14

A TRUE DEFINITION OF FAITH

Have you ever seen a little boy with a tiny toy car? Have you ever noticed what a little boy does with a little car?

He begins to dream. In fact, that little boy will "drive" that toy vehicle all over the air in front of him. He'll run you over—run that car all over your face and zoom it right over your pot-belly, if you let him.

Zooom! Brrrooom! Urrrrrrch! That kid will make all sorts of noises as if the car has a real engine that is revving up to go. He'll make noises that tell you he's braking and crashing all over the place, right in midair. His face will crinkle. He'll smile and he'll frown. That little boy with the toy car will show you, with his facial expressions, that he is going beyond merely playing . . . he's dreaming! He is putting his entire imagination to work, dreaming that he is driving that car at breakneck speed.

I consider this picture a true definition of faith. The boy has not just imagined he's driving the car; he's dreaming about it. He's sowing it into his own little heart with something Jesus called "childlike" faith. This kind of faith focuses the mind in a different way. It's open, it's innocent, and it's powerful! What that child is actually doing while he's driving that toy car in the air is this: he's plotting a course with his mind.

We call it imagination, but God wants us to use it even as adults. He gave us this ability to dream for a reason. He also gave us the ambition and the desire to do something about the dream for a reason, too. Do you think God is content for us to stay like little babies, in high chairs, swirling toy cars in the air, and dreaming for the rest of our life? NO. God wants you to grow and fulfill the dreams of your heart.

SEE IT WITH CHILDLIKE FAITH

You see, a young boy may imagine that he is driving a car at five years old, but it becomes a living reality on the day when he is finally old enough to take the driving test and get his license. It is a great day to that boy. It's a scary day for everybody else on the road!

When that boy is backing out of the driveway, his dream has come to pass. As he's getting into the fast lane, his dream of driving at breakneck speed is also coming to pass . . . whether anybody likes it or not! It's called freedom! It's called, "Let me out of this house! I've been waiting for sixteen years to drive a car. Give me some cash, Dad, because I've got places to go!"

If you're that boy's parent, it's going to seem to you like it was just yesterday when he was sitting at his high chair with spaghetti on his face, zooming a car in the air like he was on the roster at NASCAR. From that time until the moment you give him the keys, driving has been in the realm of faith. It has been a hope—a dream—and suddenly, it is at the point of manifest destiny!

I believe that God gave us a vivid imagination for a reason. He put it in us when we were still babies. Why? Because we need it! We need to dream, to imagine, to have hope and then, pure faith. It is part of who we are as human beings.

If you have a goal, you need to "see it" with the eyes of childlike faith in order for it to come to pass. Jesus put "childlike faith" as an example for us because He wants us to think with faith and creativity. It is part of the process, and it's a good part!

When we roll the idea of something over in our heads over and over again, we're dreaming. When we imagine what it will be like to walk in our destiny, we're dreaming.

When we take it a step further and actually start *"calling those things that be not as though they are"* just like Abraham, the father of faith did, then we are actually moving into a deeper level of our dreams. We're "faithing," and that's when things start moving in the spiritual realm!

SATELLITE "FAITHING"

Not long ago, Cathy came into my office and caught me looking at the ceiling and swaying my head. She looked at me like I was crazy and said, "What are you doing?"

"Satellites," I said.

"What do you mean? Jesse, what are you imagining?"

"No, Cathy, I'm having faith in its purest form. One day, we'll have one."

She just looked at me. I could see her thinking, *That boy is crazy!* But I'm not! I'm faithing! I'm faithing a satellite for our ministry because, let's face it, nobody owns space. We could broadcast the Gospel all over the world; just blanket this earth with the Good News of Jesus Christ. Glory!

How much will it cost? Millions! Can God bring it to pass? Can He give it to us? Yes! He can if we will start small and begin "faithing" like little children, putting ourselves into the dream and pulling on the manifestation with our faith. That's building a mental map on the road to divine destiny!

This is about getting an image or a picture in your mind of your dream, and about making it so clear that you can run with it. Habakkuk 2:2 says, ". . . *write the vision, and make it plain upon tables, that he may run that readeth it."* This means your vision or dream has to be plain. It needs to be written down somewhere so that you can read it . . . while running, which means *doing!*

People don't believe me when I say "crazy" things like I'm "faithing" satellites, but I don't care. Let them laugh. They couldn't believe I'd ever preach farther than Louisiana, and I've now gone all over the world. They couldn't believe that I'd ever live debt-free, but today I don't owe anybody anything but to love them. So, what do they know? They don't have my vision in front of their eyes. So, they don't have the passion for it. They don't have the faith for it.

Imagination is a human thing, but faith is a God thing. Together, they work to bring about some great results. I know that God gave me imagination for a reason. It's not just for mental stimulation and entertainment—it's also to further establish and expand the visions and dreams that He puts into my heart.

I serve a "can do" God, a God who tells me, *"I can do all things through Christ which strengtheneth me"* (Philippians 4:13). He says, *". . . with men this is impossible; but with God all things are possible"* (Matthew 19:26). He says, *". . . if thou canst believe, all things are possible to him that believeth"* (Mark 9:23).

It's so important to know that impossible dreams are God's specialty. They come to those who believe. You can laugh all you want about my "satellite faithing," but one day there will be a JDM Satellite, and then, a ring of them—so that nobody can stop the Gospel! Then, television networks will not be in the power seat. The Gospel of Jesus will be broadcast without anyone's interference or restriction. Glory! Is it impossible? Yes, and that's why it's going to happen!

You see, you have to get your mind thinking at a higher level—at the level of childlike faith. This is how you build a mental map on the road to your divine destiny. It takes more than hoping, it takes real believing—the kind that Jesus had.

Jesus spoke to the wind and waves, and they became peaceful at once. Jesus cursed the fig tree when it was not providing nourishment, and it began to shrivel up. Jesus spoke the end from the beginning—He said what He could do and what He would do. He was a man of faith, a man that built mental maps on the road to His divine destiny.

I believe that Christ wants you to do the same thing—to follow in

His footsteps and live out your destiny in faith. Say what the Father says in the Scriptures. Do what He advises in your life. The more you are joined with God in your thoughts and in your actions, the greater He is going to expand your mind for success. As with everything from God, it will start spiritually and then move to other areas of your life.

MAN WAS CREATED TO *DO* SOMETHING

You know, God didn't create this earth for us to just live bored and uninteresting lives. He wants us to live active and fulfilling lives. God gave Adam a job in the Garden, to tend to it and "dress" it, and his companion was to help him every step of the way. Notice that this was before the fall.

The need to do something is part of who we are. That's why God gave mankind a job right from the start. He knew that we needed to do something productive because He created us in His image—and He is a productive God.

We're created to be doers and not only hearers. When you act on the Word and start "pressing toward the mark" as Paul the Apostle says in Philippians 3:14, you are going to eventually get right to your appointed place. Your destiny!

God thinks the world of you. He sent His Son, Jesus, to die for you, and that was His most precious gift. That's love. That's sacrifice. Dwell on that for a while. Let God give you a revelation of His love. Because when you get a revelation of how much God cares about you, you're going to get a greater respect for yourself. Then you're going to gain a greater respect for your destiny. What an honor to be used by God, in whatever capacity!

THE ACTION OF HEARING

If you think your childlike faith isn't up to par, don't worry. You can remedy that. Romans 10:17 gives you the solution when it says, *"So then faith cometh by hearing, and hearing by the Word of God."* Notice it doesn't say faith comes by "heard." It comes by hearing.

Hearing the Word of God is something you need to do every day, because every day you'll get another opportunity to follow your divine destiny.

So, don't miss church. It's vital to your success and your destiny to hear the Word of God preached. Plus, it puts you around other people who are goaling to live more godly lives.

Read your Bible every day, not just on Sunday. The Scripture is living and active. John 1:1 tells us it is the foundation of everything when it says, *"In the beginning was the Word, and the Word was with God, and the Word was God."* That means that God is one with His own Word. So, when you become one with His Word, then you're linking yourself up to Him, and He has the power to spark your faith and send you on the right path in life.

The Word of God is what will give you the passion and the energy to move forward. If you're depressed, worn out, and don't know where to turn, turn to the Word of God. Don't think about anything in particular right then, just read. Then, study. Then, hear it preached. Let it sink into your mind and it will renew your mind, which will transform your life. But again, it's not a one-time thing.

I don't care if you've heard it before, hear it again. Figure that the act of hearing is what's going to give you that strength you need to get determined in your thoughts, your words, and your actions. It's the foundation. It's a discipline worth developing.

LINK UP WITH SOMEONE STRONG

If you've got the Word of God going into your ears, you're going to have a sharper and more in-tune mind to the pathways of God, which is going to lead you in life. It doesn't matter whether something is mental or physical, you can draw it in with faith and your will.

You may have the original thought, but if you know you can't go through with it alone, find people who can work with you to see it come to pass. They may pray with you. They may give you insight and wisdom about what to do next. The point is that they need to believe with you and they need to be strong in the areas that you are weak.

If you are a visionary, you need someone with you who is a detailed and "follow-through" kind of person. He doesn't have to have all the creative ideas. Maybe that is what you do. But he needs to be the one to help you organize those thoughts, or maybe just the paperwork!

I've got a lot of people who work with me. I can't do this ministry work alone. I need a staff of people and I need them to be detail-conscious and help me in the areas that I'm not so strong in. I need them to do the things that I either can't do as well, or don't have time to do. So, I pray for God to send me people who believe in my vision. You'll need to do the same thing.

If you are great at following through, you can bet that you're going to be hooked with somebody who isn't! That's life. We find each other because we need each other. If you want to build a house, you need someone to draw the plans. That person may not be able to lay brick, but he can sure draw! So, that's his strength. That's his skill and his talent. The bricklayer might not be able to draw a straight line, but that's okay. That's not what he's trained to do. And it takes a lot of people working together to bring a house into reality.

IT'S ALL FAITH ANYWAY

Now, let's get back to the imagination area and the faith area—that's my strength, glory to God! I like to say, "It's all faith anyway, why not believe for the impossible? Hey, anybody can believe for the possible, but I figure that I can get that on my own. Why not trust in God for the impossible? That's really using imaginative faith!"

You see, all the while that I'm "dreaming" or "imagining" my destiny, I'm actually mapping it in my mind. I'm drawing it into my future, one thought and one word at a time. I'm using the mind God gave me to focus my faith and my energy on going where God wants me to go. It is an act of my will, as well as an act of my faith.

Have you ever heard the phrase "the will to live" when some-body is in the hospital fighting a deadly sickness? The human will is powerful. The body responds to the human will to live. It responds even more when the human will is based upon God's Word, which is when faith is applied. People get healed that way miraculously. God touches their body, but His touch is drawn in by their will and their faith.

You see, broadcasting the Gospel on television was my dream but to bring it to pass, I had to get my thoughts, my faith, and my will involved.

TELEVISION CHANGED THE COURSE OF MY LIFE

As I've said so many times, television was the vehicle that brought the Gospel to me. I sure wasn't going to church . . . I was going to the club! That night, in 1974, I was in a hotel in Boston, Massachusetts, getting dressed. I was about to go and play a rock show. The TV just happened to be on . . . that's a joke, of course. My wife, Cathy, had deliberately turned the channel to Billy Graham's televised Christian Crusade.

Dr. Graham was the only preacher on TV at the time that I knew of, and the same one who I knew had led my wife to become a Christian a few years earlier. I didn't like the man. I figured he was messing things up for me by influencing my wife.

Well, I wanted to switch the station. I said something like, "I'm not watching this junk!" And my sweet little wife, who never said a bad word to me, suddenly shot back, "Why? He pulls more people than you."

She got my attention.

Now, I almost got ticked off, but then I realized the simple truth—the woman was right! I stopped long enough to listen to what the preacher had to say and, before I knew it, the love of God reached right through that television screen. It changed the path of my life forever.

That night I heard the Gospel preached like I'd never heard it preached before. I was climbing the ladder of success as a musician and doing very well financially. I thought I had it all, but in reality, I had nothing. I was going to Hell and killing my body with drugs and booze along the way. I might have been "successful," but I wasn't happy.

That night, in a hotel room in Boston, Massachusetts, I gave my life to Jesus. He came in and touched my heart. He loved me, even with booze on my breath. He didn't care that my hair was long and my heart was cold. One touch from Him changed me and set me on a new course in life—my divine destiny.

Today, I am a preacher of the Gospel and my dreams are about touching the world for Christ. I am full of joy. I've got peace of mind that I never had before. I want people to know that life can be wonderful with God.

This life is not always easy, whether you're saved or not, but with God, it is a much better life. You have hope. You have new-found ability. You have the living and active Word of God that starts changing you from the inside out, and you have the spiritual force called faith to help you create mental maps on the road to your divine destiny.

You see, I know the value of television ministry. I wasn't going to a crusade with the great Dr. Billy Graham; I was going to play a rock show. TV brings the message of Christ to the people, because sometimes the people aren't going to come to the church to hear the message of Christ—that's just a fact!

So, I figure, nobody owns space. If satellites are one way to get this Gospel preached to the whole world efficiently, then I want to do it! It may not happen this year, next year, or ten years from now, but I know that it is in my future. I figure it's all faith anyway, so I'm building a map on the road to my divine destiny to reach more and more people for the Lord Jesus Christ.

CHAPTER 15

THREE DESTINY KILLERS

GOD CAN USE anybody with the right heart, anybody who's willing to do what it takes to fulfill his divine destiny. Look at my life. Do you know where I came from? I'm a swamp boy! I've been known to have a temper, and I don't always say exactly what people think I ought to. But God isn't interested in all that! He's not grading my destiny according to my faults. When He looks at me, He sees me through a veil of His Son's sacrificial blood on the cross. He sees me at my best! He sees me through my potential "in Christ."

So, when I speak confidently about myself, I'm not bragging on me, because I can't do any of this on my own. I'm bragging on God! I'm bragging on Jesus! The One Who loved me and gave Himself for me so that I might be saved and have a life worth living.

When I look around and see what God has done through my life and my ministry, I'm amazed that God could use someone like me. No, I don't have all the elements of a typical preacher, but that's all right! My ministry is proof positive that God can work with anyone, as long as that person has the right heart, and that He doesn't mind diversity in skin color, in speech, in methods, and in many other areas. The only area He will not compromise on isn't found in personal quirks or in culture, but in the heart.

DESTINY KILLER #1: SECURITY IN EARTHLY THINGS

There are some destiny-killing heart issues that you may have to deal with—areas in your life that have the potential to rob you of God's best for your life. One of the most memorable stories in the Bible that illustrates this point is the story of the Rich Young Ruler. Unlike Peter, who had personality issues that needed to be worked out, the Rich Young Ruler had a destiny-killing heart issue that stumped his potential.

You've heard me quote Mark 10:27 many times: *". . . with men it is impossible, but not with God; for with God all things are possible."* But, did you know that this great statement was made by Jesus right after his encounter with the Rich Young Ruler?

Take a look at this story with me a little closer. I want you to notice that this boy was rich, young, and seeking out Jesus. In Mark 10:17, the Bible says that he sought Christ out to ask one very important question: *". . . Good Master, what shall I do that I may inherit eternal life?"*

Picture the scene. The Bible says this young man was kneeling on the ground, looking up at Jesus, when he heard this answer: *"Thou knowest the commandments, Do not commit adultery, Do not kill, Do not steal, Do not bear false witness, Defraud not, Honour thy father and mother"* (Mark 10:19).

Now, he was looking directly into the face of the Son of God, who could spot a lie a mile away . . . and do you know what the boy said? *"Master, all these have I observed from my youth"* (Mark 10:20).

Have you ever met *anybody* who observed *all* the commandments from his youth? I haven't! I don't know anyone who has done right *all* his life. The teenage years alone mess up most people! Yet, Jesus didn't argue with the young man.

It reminds me of that commercial on television where you see a guy who is surfing the web and he hears a message that says something like, "You have now finished the Internet. Press ESCAPE to go back." I mean, that's almost impossible, isn't it?! Yet, this Rich Young Ruler could say that from the time he was born until this point with Christ, he'd observed *everything* Jesus said in the passage. Look at what the Word says next.

"Then Jesus beholding him loved him . . ." It blessed Jesus to look into the face of one who cared so much about God. *". . . and said unto him, One thing thou lackest: go thy way, sell whatsoever thou hast, and give to the poor, and thou shalt have treasure in heaven: and come, take up the cross, and follow Me"* (Mark 10:21).

Now, Jesus rarely said, "Take up the cross and follow Me." Most of the time, when people tried to follow Him, Jesus said something like, "Go and tell people the great things God has done for you." But not this boy, and I believe it is because Jesus wanted the Rich Young Ruler on His staff.

This young man could have been a disciple. Think about it. He was rich and knew how to handle money; He loved God and obeyed all the commandments. Remember, Jesus knew Judas was stealing from Him. Maybe Jesus figured, "Hey, I've got a good replacement right here!" But something messed it all up—a hidden weakness.

Jesus shined a light on this man's weakness when He said, *". . . One thing thou lackest: go thy way, sell whatsoever thou hast, and give to the poor. . . ."* You see, Jesus spotted something that He wanted to deliver the boy from. **This Rich Young Ruler's greatest weakness was that his main security was in earthly things** and not in the Lord.

At that moment, Jesus gave the young ruler an opportunity to change his ways. He gave him an opportunity to conquer his weakness. The Rich Young Ruler had a choice to make.

Now, this young man could have made the greatest investment of his life. He could have given away his possessions and walked with Jesus Christ in His earthly ministry; he could have been there when

Jesus preached, delivered, and healed the masses. Yet, he passed up that divine opportunity.

DESTINY KILLER #2: LACK OF TRUST

Personally, I believe that Jesus would have seen to it that he was financially blessed beyond what he'd given up for the sake of the call. After all, read Mark 10:29–30: *"And Jesus answered and said, 'Verily I say unto you, There is no man that hath left house, or brethren, or sisters, or father, or mother, or wife, or children, or lands, for My sake, and the Gospel's, But he shall receive an hundredfold now in this time, houses, and brethren, and sisters, and mothers, and children, and lands, with persecutions; and in the world to come eternal life.'"*

Notice that those who give up so much for Christ's sake and the Gospel's sake are rewarded a *"hundredfold now in this time,"* as well as *"in the world to come eternal life."* So, the Rich Young Ruler really didn't have anything to lose, although he didn't see it that way.

This was an issue of trust, an issue of security. I also believe that He wanted the Rich Young Ruler to be a disciple, but He first wanted him to get his priorities straight. That young man's security had to be in the right place.

The boy could not do it. The Bible says, *"And he was sad at that saying, and went away grieved: for he had great possessions"* (Mark 10:22).

The Rich Young Ruler got up from his knees and left. He forsook the call of God on his life, and the Bible says he grieved because he had great possessions. What was he grieving over? Not his money, because he still had that. I believe He grieved over his loss, over his inability to trust Jesus and, ultimately, I believe he grieved over "what could have been." Because, you see, **the Rich Young Ruler kept his money, but he gave up his destiny.**

Mark 10:23 gives us Jesus's response: *"And Jesus looked round about, and saith unto His disciples, How hardly shall they that have riches enter into the kingdom of God!"*

This young man's lack of trust in the Lord as his Provider

killed his destiny. It totally shot his chances of truly following after Jesus.

DESTINY KILLER #3: THE LOVE OF MONEY

Some people read this story and think it's all about money. It's not. That day, after the Rich Young Ruler had left, Jesus took the opportunity to teach His disciples a lesson.

You see, they *had* trusted in Jesus and followed Him into the ministry. But, **unlike the Rich Young Ruler, none of the disciples had been told to sell all their earthly possessions. They were told to *follow* Christ but *not* to sell what they had and give it to the poor.**

So, the disciples were shocked to hear Jesus's comment about it being difficult to enter into the kingdom with riches.

Mark 10:24–26 of the Amplified Bible says they were, *". . . amazed and bewildered and perplexed at His words. But Jesus said to them again, Children, how hard it is for those who trust (place their confidence, their sense of safety) in riches to enter the kingdom of God! It is easier for a camel to go through the eye of a needle than for a rich man to enter the kingdom of God. And they were shocked and exceedingly astonished, and said to Him and to one another, Then who can be saved?"*

Why were the disciples so astonished? (1) Because they *weren't* poor! They were like the camels Jesus talked about! (2) They thought Jesus was talking about Heaven, but He wasn't.

Now, had the disciples been poor, they would have been thrilled about the camel and the needle comment. They'd have thought, *Praise God, we're so poor we're definitely going to make it!* But, no! The Scriptures show us that they were floored, and verse 26 sums up their feelings best when it says, *"Then who can be saved?"*

Peter probably thought, *Oh, man, we're going to have to sell the boats if we want to fit through that needle!*

Peter never did get fully out of the fishing business because after Jesus was crucified, he said, "I go a-fishing!" He went back to his business. The truth is that those on Jesus's staff were businesspeople.

He had an accountant, a tax guy, and a few guys who owned fishing businesses, too. They all had some money, but they were following Jesus and trusting in Him first.

I did some research and found out that, in Jesus's day, the only people who paid taxes were people of wealth. Jesus's temple tax would have been thirty percent, and Judas was stealing for three years without any of the other disciples knowing. If you think Jesus looked poor, think again. They gambled for His clothes when He was on the cross and nobody gambles for rags.

Jesus knew that it was an economic world. He didn't ask everyone who followed Him to sell everything they had and give it to the poor. Jesus had money, and He used it just like everyone else, to eat, live, and give. But His trust was in God and He wanted those who followed Him to put their trust in God, too. The Rich Young Ruler's three main problems were that (1) his security was in earthly things (2) he didn't fully trust the Lord and, (3) he hid a love of money in his heart.

1 Timothy 6:10 puts it best when it says, *"For the love of money is the root of all evil: which while some coveted after, they have erred from the faith, and pierced themselves through with many sorrows."*

It doesn't say that money is the root of all evil; it says the *love* of money is the root of all evil. Notice that this love pierces a person with sorrow—sounds a lot like the Rich Young Ruler, doesn't it? The love of money is a destiny-killer.

KINGDOM OF GOD OR KINGDOM OF HEAVEN?

People misunderstand the camel-and-the-needle parable and assume that Jesus was talking about Heaven. But He was talking about the Kingdom of *God,* and it's an entirely different thing! The Kingdom of God is a method; the Kingdom of Heaven is a place. The Kingdom of God is His way of doing things on the earth. The Kingdom of Heaven is a place where we're going to spend eternity!

The Amplified Bible better explains the Kingdom of God when

it says this: *"But seek (aim at and strive after) first of all His kingdom and His righteousness (His way of doing and being right), and then all these things taken together will be given you besides"* (Matthew 6:33).

God's way of doing things and being right is what you should strive toward. Now, go back and read Mark 10:24, *". . . how hard is it for them that trust in riches to enter into the kingdom of God!"* It makes better sense then, doesn't it?!

It is very hard for a man who puts his trust in riches to do things God's way. His money has priority over God. His trust is in the security that his material things give him.

It's not hard for poor people to trust God, because they don't have anything else to trust in, but rich people have more options. That's why Jesus could say that. But material things will pass away. It's only God and His Word that will never pass away.

To please Him, we must have faith in Him and put Him first. Look at Mark 4:30 and you'll hear Jesus further explaining the kingdom of God. He doesn't talk about Heaven. There, Jesus compares God's kingdom—His way of doing things—to sowing seed because He knows that life is about giving and receiving. It is a continual exchange between people.

In the Mark 4 parable, Jesus tells you that if you will do things God's way, it's as if you are planting seeds that will eventually grow into large branches for other living things to rest upon. You see, God's way of doing things helps you to grow in life and become strong and secure—like a mighty branch!

Jesus's words about Him being the vine and we being the branches flows right along with this. When we do things His way, needy people will seek us out because they know we're strong enough to hold them up. We're rooted in the permanence of our God! That enables us to help others make it to the Kingdom of Heaven *and* show them how to start doing things God's way upon the earth.

PERFECT LOVE CASTS OUT ALL FEAR

Money is a touchy subject with people. Yet God asks His people to bring the first-fruits into the church. God says that the tithe—a tenth of our income—belongs to Him, yet many believers just won't tithe, even though the Bible says God will open up the windows of Heaven and bless those who give with more than they can contain. Giving is part of God's system of getting prosperity to you, not *from* you.

Do you know why so many believers don't give God His due, the tithe? It doesn't have a thing to do with money. It's because their love is not perfected and fear of lack is still ruling their lives. It's a trust issue.

1 John 4:18 says, *"There is no fear in love; but perfect love casteth out fear: because fear hath torment.* **He that feareth is not made perfect in love.***"*

For people who don't tithe, the fear of losing the security they feel from having money has gripped them to a point that they are too scared to give. They already have so much "month" at the end of their "money" that they don't know how in the world they'll ever be able to give and to pay the bills! That's fear at work, and even though it sounds wise, natural, in this case to cut God first, it isn't, because it's like eating the seed when what you really need is a crop!

Fear is at the center of all trust issues, and it's why some people won't take the opportunity God gives them to tithe no matter how much Scripture they hear about being blessed. Their love is simply not perfected in that area. They don't know that God loves them enough to really come through in keeping them safe and secure. There is a battle going on, an inner struggle between a sincere love for God and the fear of losing personal security. It's the same battle the Rich Young Ruler fought and lost.

It's a fear-based life, instead of a faith-based life that says, "I *can't* give to God." I've seen it happen so many times that those who choose to put God first, to put their security in Him and tithe, end up having more money than they have "month." **A reversal starts happening.**

God's Word cannot and will not return void. Galatians 6:7 says it best, *"Be not deceived; God is not mocked: for whatsoever a man soweth, that shall he also reap."* Blessing follows those who put their trust in God.

RACISM IS ABOUT FEAR

Here's another issue that is based in fear and can kill your destiny—racism! Racism is a form of fear and hatred, and it's totally against God's way of doing things. If you want to succeed and fulfill your divine destiny with joy, then you've got to get along with other people in this life—and they may not all have your same color skin or your same culture. Look, God made each of us, and He likes us!

But let's face it. I've met many white men who would lose their mind if their lily-white daughter wanted to marry a black guy. They'd be on their knees saying, "Oh, God! What am I going to do! What's the baby going to look like, oh, Jesus!"

Racism is about fear—fear of what other people will think and say, fear that the "good" genes will be squashed out, fear that somebody different in look and in culture is going to end up related to them!

Black people are no different when it comes to this. If a mixed couple has a baby, most black grandpas are praying the baby comes out dark. The white grandpas are praying the baby comes out light. Everybody wants their kids and grandkids coming out looking like their side of the family and acting like them! Why? They are the most comfortable and the least fearful around people who are similar to them.

To me, racism is first about fear. It's about trying to conquer that fear by acting superior, by wanting to control and suppress others. Everything else becomes an offshoot of the initial fear that sparks racism.

As believers, God gives us the answer to getting rid of our fears in life and it's through the perfecting nature of His love. His love helps us to be at peace in ourselves, and not be intimidated by other people. His love opens our mind and gives us a desire to understand others and not judge others. His love stamps out racism in our mind and helps us to live at peace with those who have a different culture, background, and skin color than us.

When you build a mental map on the road to your divine destiny, don't think that the road is only going to be filled with people who look just like you—because it probably won't! God wants you to broaden how you think. Your destiny is going to stretch you beyond your comfort zone, so you might as well start getting flexible now!

Adopt a "seek and destroy" mind-set when it comes to fear. Don't let any of that trash hinder you from being who you are in Christ. Fear is the enemy. Satan is the enemy. If you have problems with this area, bring it to God. Let Him shine a light on your weak spots, like He did with the Rich Young Ruler. Then release the fear to Him. Let Him give you a spirit of love that casts out ALL fear—fear of loss, fear of other cultures, and fear of anything that would kill your divine destiny.

Ephesians 6:12 tells us plainly that people are never our problem: *"For we wrestle not against flesh and blood, but against principalities, against powers, against the rulers of the darkness of this world, against spiritual wickedness in high places."*

Fear is rooted in darkness, but as children of God, we've been delivered from that! Colossians 1:13 says it best, *"Who hath delivered us from the power of darkness, and hath translated us into the kingdom of His dear Son."*

Love, trust, and faith are all key elements in reaching your destiny. Don't forsake them. They are part of God's kingdom ways—part of what's going to keep you running straight down the road to your divine destiny!

GOD CAN USE ANYBODY

In life, we can sometimes think that God can only use certain kinds of people, but God often picks the most unlikely people to do His work. Look at His disciples. They were a mixed bag of men. Some were educated beyond belief and others were simple fishermen. The Bible we read today was penned by all different types of believers, all used by God to give us His Word!

Peter was a fire-and-brimstone kind of preacher. He'd cuss you, cut you, and repent later. He also betrayed Jesus. Was he the kind of guy that you'd think God would use to build His church? If you and I were picking names out of a hat and pulled Peter's, we'd put it right back in! Yet, God saw the man's heart. He saw beyond his personality problems. In Matthew 16:15, Jesus asked Peter, *". . . But who say ye that I am?"* It was Peter who said, *". . . Thou art the Christ, the Son of the living God."*

This man, although not perfect, was spirit-led in many ways, and Jesus pegged his destiny in Matthew 16:17–19: *"And Jesus answered and said unto him, Blessed art thou, Simon Barjona: for flesh and blood hath not revealed it unto thee, but My Father which is in heaven. And I say also unto thee, That thou art Peter, and upon this rock I will build My church; and the gates of hell shall not prevail against it."*

Jesus built His church with Peter as the leader. Peter was an unlikely man with an unlikely destiny, but with Jesus as his "rock"—his immovable and powerful Cornerstone—not even Hell itself could prevail!

GOD BELIEVES IN YOU. DO YOU?

Jesus believed in Peter. He believes in you, too. When you get a revelation of that, you are going to gain greater confidence in yourself. You're going to start seeing that, even though you're not perfect, God can use you.

There is nothing that you can't do. Remember, you were made in God's image and in His likeness—from the beginning of time, your very being was made in God's image. What *is* His image? Is it fearful? Is it directionless? Is it worried about the devil? No! We serve a God who is fearless and focused, and He is the One who sent His only Son to beat the devil—as a man.

Do you realize that the Christ you serve didn't even use His heavenly powers to defeat the devil? He did it as a mortal man. When Jesus went to the cross, He went as a blameless and sinless man—a pure sacrifice. The sins of the world were hung on Him. He took our grief, sorrow, and shame. He wore every horrific sin on His body on that cross. He paid the price so that we didn't have to—so that we could be saved and be made free!

Today, the work of the cross is finished. It's a done deal. We don't have to earn our salvation. It's a free gift that we accept by grace. We also don't have to earn our authority in Christ. It has been given to us by way of the cross. Now, all we have to do is walk in that authority, or in other words, trust in the work of the cross.

Peter had an incredible destiny to build the church. How could he do it? He had to do it "in Christ." He had to die to himself and live through Christ. You see, in Christ, you are strong. In Christ, you are bold. In Christ, you have love, joy, peace, and patience. In Christ, you have everything you need to live this life and fulfill your own personal destiny.

Peter's destiny took personal traits that only he possessed. Your destiny will also take traits that only you possess. God knows that you have exactly what's needed to fulfill your divine destiny.

CHAPTER 16

GREATEST WEAKNESS OR GREATEST DESIRE? LUST GONE TOO FAR

YOUR GREATEST WEAKNESS will stop your greatest desire. Many men and women in the Bible and in modern times have seen their greatest desire destroyed by one thing—personal weakness.

Leaders have lost their dream of higher office simply because of a weakness.

Preachers have lost their reputation and integrity simply because of a weakness.

Businesspeople who would have seen great success lost it all simply because of a weakness.

Weaknesses—we all have them. It's how we handle them that makes the difference in life. You see, attacks will come. Temptations will arise. The devil will make sure of it. He will rarely attack you in your strong area because he knows that he doesn't have a good chance of causing you to fail or fall in that area. He's looking for a weak spot, somewhere he can put the pressure on you to fail.

Your destiny in this life isn't to get near your "greatest desire" and blow it! Your destiny is to live out your life with joy, overcoming obstacles, but not being a slave to anything!

If there is a "greatest weakness" plaguing your life—something that wants to enslave you—then it's best to start working on that area now so that it doesn't rob you of what you really want in life, your greatest desire.

LET THE WEAK *SAY* I AM STRONG

The first thing you need to work on is your mouth. Whatever your weakness in life, search the Word for a Scripture that you can stand on and then, start confessing strength. Start speaking it out. Your words are part of your mental map. Let Joel 3:10 be your guide: "*. . . let the weak say, I am strong."*

The weak must *say* that they are strong because voicing strength is crucial to getting strength. So, when you're strong, *say* you're strong. When you're weak, *say* you're strong. I'm not talking about ignoring your weaknesses. This is not about denial; it's about taking charge and using the Word to cut away the weakness. Talk STRONG!

Now, the flip side is that if you just ignore your weakness, you will not get any better at overcoming it. In fact, what you're really doing when you don't deal with a weakness is this: you're mentally indulging in your weakness.

If you do this enough, it will cause you to stumble throughout your life. If you let that weakness run your mind, it will run your life. Your greatest weakness will eventually cause you to forfeit your greatest desire. It will create a "past" that will hinder your future. It will stop your destiny just like it stopped the Rich Young Ruler's.

In the previous chapter, we saw how the Rich Young Ruler wanted nothing more than to do right by God. That's why he could say he'd observed all the commandments from his youth. Yet he couldn't follow Jesus and become a disciple because he hadn't dealt with his weakness. Deal with your weaknesses now so that you don't lose out on the destiny that is coming to you!

Remember, Jesus may call you to do something really big for Him, but it won't matter how much He calls you if you've got a weakness that you aren't willing to give up. The Rich Young Ruler heard the voice of God saying "follow Me," but he couldn't do it any more than he could fly around the moon because he wasn't willing to give up his greatest weakness. Don't let that happen to you.

WHO IS YOUR EXAMPLE FOR MORALITY—DAVID?

In the Bible, there was a boy named David who became a king—and his life is an example of both greatness and weakness. His is an example that you can learn from, but that you should not try to replicate. The Bible is full of stories about various people, some who were geniuses and some who were near to fools. But none should be looked up to but Jesus.

David, as you probably know if you've read the Bible story, had a problem with women. Today, many men in the ministry—and public office and many other arenas—use David as a crutch. If they fall repeatedly to temptation, they don't really feel sorry about it. Instead, they consider themselves like a modern David—gifted and anointed by God, but with a weakness. That's a messed-up way of thinking. God wants you to set your standards higher. David isn't your Jesus! So, don't treat him like he is.

When people use David as their example, I get ticked off! Why bring a biblical man into the mix? Just take responsibility for it, ask for forgiveness, repent, and move on. Don't drag King David into your problems. He had enough of his own!

Look, I don't care if David was a man after God's own heart, the man still isn't supposed to be our example of morality. That boy's story is in the Bible for many reasons and you can learn a lot from reading about his life, but the lesson to learn from David when it comes to women is pretty clear—here is what NOT to do.

Going through women like they're sexual objects was David's problem—a problem he indulged too long. So, reading about his life and admiring him for his other great talents is not an excuse to act just like him when it comes to his sexual promiscuity. That was his weak area. He indulged it because, well, he could. He was king and nobody would stop him. But that weakness, that total unrestraint, did a lot of harm in his life.

If you're saved and keep running around with women, and you use David as an excuse for your own immorality, you are frustrating the grace of God—plain and simple. Can you be forgiven? Yes. Of course, you'll draw on the grace of God. But, there is a higher life for you and a better destiny.

AIM HIGHER

Why not take your goal-setting to a higher level? Why not focus on Jesus, the King of Kings? Nobody walks around asking themselves, "What would David do?" If he does, he's a fool.

You can't base your life on people. People will fail. They'll disappoint you. Jesus never failed. So, His life is the highest in rank. If you're going to live this Christianity, aim higher. Think well of yourself.

Build yourself a mental map that says, "My body is a temple and I will be holy. I can't be perfect in moment, but I can be holy in a moment. I'm not an animal driven by every thought that comes into my mind. I cast down thoughts to the obedience of Christ and I chose a higher path in life."

You determine what you are going to do. Don't let another man's weakness determine what you're going to do. That can mess up your mental map and steer you off course in life. Let Jesus be your example for living, because He didn't have a problem with women and He finished His destiny without regret.

JESUS—TEMPTED BUT DESTINY-BOUND

In a time when women were treated like dogs, Jesus lifted women up. He didn't see women as sexual objects to conquer. He saw them as human beings in need of a Savior. He considered women strong, precious, and worthy of love and not objectification; to be cherished, loved, and forgiven—not used or abused.

Jesus had a lot of women following Him. He even had a prostitute as a convert, but He didn't use her or abuse her. He saved her and set her free! In fact, she was one of the women at the tomb who was honored to be the first to find out about Christ's resurrection. Christ honored His mother. He was friends with women. Women were some of His greatest supporters. Remember Mary and Martha?

In my years in ministry, I've seen firsthand that women are naturally more sensitive to the things of God. They are often quicker to have faith in God, quicker to show mercy, and quicker to repent when they need to. They are precious gifts to the body of Christ.

Why is it so hard for people to see Jesus as sexually pure? Because they base what He did on their own standards . . . and they aren't shooting too high!

For many people, the idea of Jesus remaining sexually pure while surrounded by women is mind-boggling. Ever since Christianity began, people have been trying to get their minds around it. They don't understand it. They couldn't do it themselves. So, they end up jumping to conclusions, warping history, and soiling the reputation of Jesus based on their own ideas about sexuality and their own view of what a man can and cannot do . . . but man's ideas never determine God's ways! Jesus was on a whole other level!

Jesus remained sexually pure, according to the Word . . . but that doesn't mean He walked around in a fog and wasn't sexually tempted. The Word says that He was tempted "in all points" just like we are, but he still didn't fall.

Hebrews 4:15–16 says, *"For we have not an High Priest which cannot be touched with the feeling of our infirmities; but was in all points tempted like as we are, yet without sin. Let us therefore come boldly unto the throne of grace, that we may obtain mercy, and find grace to help in time of need."*

Temptation after temptation after temptation, Christ made the right choices for His life and His destiny. He knew He only had so much time on this earth and He had a job to do. He came to this earth to save mankind. He had a purpose, a destiny, to fulfill. And His destiny was something that went beyond human sexuality. It went into spirituality, a purer and higher form of living.

None of us will ever be Jesus, there can only be One. But He is still our example for living, in that our aim should be higher and purer.

That Scripture in Hebrews 4:15 shows us that Jesus understands. He knows how we feel because He's been there. He knows what it is like to be tempted and what it is like to make the right turn in life in order to fulfill a destiny—and all of us have a destiny to fulfill.

Some people are priests and feel called of God to celibacy, but most of us are not called to that life. In the very beginning of the Bible, God tells us that it is not good for man to be alone. Genesis 2:18 says, *"And the LORD God said, It is not good that the man should be alone; I will make him an help meet for him."* That is when woman was introduced to man, and God saw it as a very, very good thing.

There is nothing wrong with sex. It's God-created. But there is something wrong with abuse and objectification. All of us are tempted, but we can pray to Christ and ask Him to impart strength to us to overcome whatever is in our way, just as He did.

Some people think that it's impossible to overcome a sexual weakness, but it's not. Jesus did it and that means that we can, too.

Jesus lived a sinless and blameless life because, before the foundation of the world, He knew that His destiny was to be the Lamb slain. Our eternity depended on Christ sticking to His divine destiny. Thank God, He did!

David, however, is a perfect example of how a person's weakness can stop his greatest desire—can even alter God's best plan for our life. Yes, David was a good man, a man after God's own heart. But in his later years, he lost out on something that he desperately wanted to do, all because of his greatest weakness, and that same weakness caused repercussions in his family for years.

The point is that, if you have built a mental map toward a particular goal, but you allow a weakness in your character to run unchecked, it will eventually take something from you that you really want . . . and you will be sorely disappointed by what "could have" been.

Regret is a terrible thing. It eats people up inside. So, if you can avoid it, why not? If you have a weakness in this area, learn to conquer it before it destroys your potential. I don't know your destiny or your path in life, but God does, and if you turn to Him—in every instance you're tempted—He can help you escape that temptation and keep moving forward toward His best.

DAVID'S DESTINY—KING!

Insecurity breeds problems. I believe that David's weakness was born out of insecurity—something that can also hinder your mental map and it can sure hinder your actions.

Insecurity can steal opportunities right out from under your nose because it can make you give up what you really want. Insecurity can also breed that "greatest weakness."

Let's back up a bit and talk about David's beginnings and explore how he got to be such a womanizer. Okay, when God took the kingdom of Israel away from King Saul, He told the priest, Samuel, to start looking for a new king by searching the house of Jesse. David was one of Jesse's boys.

So, Jesse asked seven of his sons to come out and stand before the priest, Samuel. They all looked good and old Sam was excited! He especially liked the firstborn named Eliad. That boy *looked* like a king! Plus, he was the firstborn, which gave him an edge in the family.

But God knew that Samuel had messed up the first time by picking Saul according to his outward appearance. Saul was tall, but that doesn't mean anything! A true king has the right stuff on the *inside,* not necessarily on the outside!

God wanted the man with the right heart, and He didn't move upon Samuel to anoint any one of the seven sons that Jesse had presented to him. Samuel was confused. He knew that God told him to anoint a son of Jesse's, but he knew none of those boys fit the bill. So, he did the only thing he knew to do. He asked Jesse if there were any other sons.

Jesse said, and this is my paraphrase of the story, "Well, we got one more boy . . . but we don't let him come in the house much. He's a musician and he's a little strange. Sings to sheep. He's a poet who doesn't know it." That's right. Jesse totally disregarded his son. He didn't even bother to put him in a line with his other sons. That is rejection, and it breeds insecurity.

Look in the Bible and you'll see. You very seldom find David inside his father's house. You also never hear David's mother speaking about him. Why? I believe it was because David was considered unimportant to the family. They disregarded him.

When Samuel heard Jesse had another son, he said, "Bring the boy to me." Jesse went and got David. That priest, Samuel, took one look at David and God spoke to his heart.

1 Samuel 16:7 says, *"But the LORD said unto Samuel, Look not on his countenance, or on the height of his stature; because I have refused him: for the LORD seeth not as man seeth; for man looketh on the outward appearance, but the LORD looketh on the heart."*

Notice that God chose a person nobody thought of—nobody regarded—not even his own family. God told Samuel, and I'm paraphrasing again, "Don't look at his height. Don't look at his face. I've already looked at his heart and that boy is your king!"

David was anointed, but his family didn't know it. You may be like David. God may have given you a talent, a dream, a concept that He wants you to flow in and develop in your life. He may have anointed you to do something, but nobody may be able to see it, not even those closest to you.

Do not let their blindness to your goodness or your gifting draw you into insecurity. God is with you! He sees what's inside you, even if nobody else does. You may not look the part. You may be rejected and dismissed. But God is on your side. Pray for a Samuel in your life, someone who will be Spirit-led and notice the gift of God on your life. Then, just live and know that your destiny comes day by day and step by step.

David wasn't crowned king that day, although he was anointed that day! Remember that. Don't give up. Your time will come and you will step into history at just the right moment. Until then, develop your strengths. Conquer your weakness. When you see insecurity driving you to do something you don't want to do, notice it. Don't follow through with your weakness. If you do this, when you're crowned "king" you won't have to hobble along with that weakness strapped to your back like David did.

DESIRE ROBBED BY WEAKNESS

David's weakness for women went unchecked throughout his reign. After all, he was king and he could do whatever he wanted. The Bible says that David had beautiful eyes, and you know how women *love* eyes. Men don't care if a woman's blind—they're looking at other parts or they're seeing her as a whole—but women love to look into a man's eyes!

David's penetrating stare was what got him in trouble. There is a lesson in this. Watch yourself! What has your gaze? What has your attention? Is it something that will profit you or harm you?

If you let a distraction go on too long, it will become a main attraction in your life . . . and will steal your focus. Without focus, you can't build a mental map. Without a mental map, you don't have the determination to make the next step. Your ideas will stop cold. You'll be inactive. Why? It starts with thoughts. So, watch what you're looking at.

David couldn't look away when he caught sight of a woman named Bathsheba. And because he never stopped gazing, his mind never stopped wandering. He never put his weakness in check and so, lust eventually drove him to commit a crime—the worst crime— murder (2 Samuel 11–12). Now, I know this is an extreme example, but it makes a real good point!

Just listen to this mess! David saw Bathsheba bathing. He lusted after her and had her brought to him so that he could sleep with her. He knew she was married but he didn't care and, as the king, Bathsheba had no other choice but to allow him to have his way with her. She got pregnant and sent word to David about it.

David made a decision to kill the woman's husband, Uriah the Hittite, so he could take her as his wife. Is that a kick in the head? Now, Uriah was in David's army and a battle was going on. David gave instructions that would have Uriah placed deliberately on the front lines of battle so that he would die.

He sent Uriah to battle to die just because he wanted his woman—a woman he'd already slept with. Now, that was a completely selfish crime, a ruthless killing, motivated by lust and facilitated by power. The point? Sometimes a weakness creates a scenario that just builds and builds. The deeper you entangle yourself, the deeper you go into sin, and you end up doing things you never thought you would do.

David didn't wake up one day and say, "Hmm, I think I'll kill Uriah today. His wife looks pretty good." No, it started small. It started when he couldn't take his eyes off the woman while she was washing up. Everything starts small. Sin starts small. But if you give that weakness an inch, it will take a mile out of your life . . . and maybe somebody else's, too.

LUST AND MURDER FOLLOWED HIS CHILDREN

Was David repentant? Yes! We know that the Bible says that David was truly repentant and God even forgave him for the murder, but that didn't mean that there weren't consequences. What David sowed, he reaped. He basically had Uriah killed and, in return, the baby he had fathered with Bathsheba got sick and died.

Now, here's another lesson you can learn. Weakness will pass down generation to generation until somebody stops it. It will rob even your children from experiencing God's best in their lives.

The Bible gives insight into some of David's other children, who went on to have problems with what? You guessed it, sex and killing. One of his sons raped one of his daughters—sexual misconduct, another instance of lust gone unchecked—and then refused to marry her, which was standard in that time. In that time, if it was known that the sister wasn't a virgin, no other man would want to marry her. So, he not only raped her but he also stole her future. She was distraught.

Her daddy, David, who could have done something to rectify it, did nothing. He let it go because he loved his son—another sign that even his own daughters were not important in his sight. Love should never be an excuse not to discipline. That's misguided parenting that only hurts the child's future. So, David was lenient with sexual immorality.

Because he didn't do anything about the rape, another one of his sons got ticked off. He took revenge on the rapist and murdered him in cold blood. So, David had a death in the family on his hands, a death that began with unchecked lust. Guess what? He let that slide, too. David understood and forgave that son, which was fine, but he also let the son's pride continue to swell.

That same son eventually turned against David, stealing the heart of many of David's people and deceiving him. They ended up going to battle against each other—and twenty thousand people were killed in that battle, one of which was the son. It broke David's heart.

Now, if that's not a dysfunctional family, I don't know what is! David was a man after God's own heart in some ways, but his family life stunk to high heaven with sin and leniency.

Do you see how David's problems followed his children? Lust, left unchecked, not only can destroy your life, but it can destroy many lives. What you don't nip in the bud will go on.

Your children learn from your example, bad or good. What you neglect to teach them or what you neglect to enforce can cause a ripple effect of pain down the road. Some types of children will see what you do and say, "I never want to be like that," but others will follow right in your footsteps, which may not be the best place for them to go. Don't send them the wrong message. If you love them, live your life for God and let them see you making strides to conquer what is standing in your way.

No matter how talented or anointed you are, if you let a weakness run wild, it will crash-course your mental map. It will lead you, and possibly those you love, down roads you don't want to travel . . . and those are always windy and dysfunctional roads! Roads that just might veer you far away from your greatest desire.

DAVID'S GREATEST DESIRE

The Bible tells us that King David had the plans for an amazing temple on his heart (1 Chronicles 28:11–19). He wanted to build something spectacular, and he wanted to do it more than he wanted to do anything else in life. What did God say about it? He said, and again I'm paraphrasing, "David, you can't build My house."

"But why?" David said, "The plans are on my heart!"

"Because you have blood on your hands."

David had Uriah's innocent blood on his hands, and although he was forgiven, it hindered him from doing what he really wanted to do. I believe that the crime had many consequences, as you've read, but the one that really bothered David the most was that he couldn't fulfill his greatest desire—to build the most beautiful temple anyone had ever seen to honor God. David was a doer. He wanted his reign to end by building something magnificent for God, but God would not let him do it.

Oh, the temple still got built and it was glorious, but David wasn't the king who got it done. The job was passed to Solomon, David's son—a man who would become known as the wisest and the richest man in the history of the world.

David's greatest weakness stopped his greatest desire.

Have you determined to be focused in your thoughts? Are you a doer? If so, you have great potential. Let all these lessons from David's life show you how important it is to make the right choices in your life.

Nothing is worth losing your greatest desire over. No weakness is worth damaging your life or the future of your kids. Remember, you can have the best and most determined mental map. You can have the best ideas and the best concepts, ones that will revolutionize the way people live, work, and worship.

You can be the most active doer that you know and see great success in your life . . . but if you let lust run your life, it will eventually erode your joy in life and it will steal what you really want the most. It will cause the realization of your greatest desire to be passed along to someone else.

CHAPTER 17

GREATEST WEAKNESS OR GREATEST DESIRE? JUDAS AND THE LOVE OF MONEY

THE LOVE OF money is another great weakness that many people have. This one steals just as much, if not more, than lust. It's a weakness that may drive you to succeed at whatever the personal cost, but it can also kill you and steal everything you really need right out from under your nose.

Now, don't get me wrong. Wealth is a good thing. It's a blessing from God. You can't eat without it, and you need to eat! This is an economic world we're living in, that's a fact, and there is nothing wrong with prosperity. Read your Bible and you'll see that riches and honor followed those who loved God and obeyed His commands.

Even God Himself said that He takes pleasure in seeing us prosper (Psalm 35:27). Don't get hung up on the logistics of what's "too much" and what's "appropriate." You're serving a God Who uses gold like it's concrete and pearl like it's iron for His gates . . . so, don't think that God really gives a flip about you having what other people might deem "too much."

YOU CAN'T OUT-BLING GOD

You can't fathom the prosperity of Heaven. On your best day, you can't impress God with your wealth. I don't care how much you're blinging, it's nothing by comparison to Heaven or the riches in Glory.

So, you can't impress God with your wealth, even on your best day. Think about it. God put diamonds in the earth right next to regular rocks. He filled this earth with riches, some of which we consider valuable and others that we don't.

God loves it all because He created it all, and He wants to bless you with what *you* like—regardless if it is a paper necklace or a diamond ring. God loves you and wants you to believe the best, to have faith, and to put your trust in Him so that He can lead you in life.

The only problem when it comes to money is that God doesn't want you to love it . . . He wants your love to be reserved for Him and for other people, and not for something as fleeting as money.

You see, you can't think with determination, you can't talk with faith, or walk along destiny's good path when you're hanging on to a weakness like the love of money. Judas is a perfect example of that.

JUDAS'S GREATEST WEAKNESS—LOVE OF MONEY

Money isn't bad in and of itself. If it was, Jesus would never have had a treasurer. That was Judas's job. So, if you think Christ was poor, what's the point of having a guy on staff to handle your money if you don't have any. Let the elevator go to the top!

The *love* of money—which is greed—and the notion that you can actually put something as valuable as your trust in money is what is at odds with Christianity.

Let's look at Judas as an example of how the love of money can rob you of a godly mental map and a long life. Today, most people just think of Judas as a thief, but in actuality, I believe that Judas was really a great man . . . a great man with an unchecked weakness. Because he eventually betrayed Jesus, most people think that Judas lived his life as a distant disciple. That's not true. Jesus was extremely close to this disciple, just as He was with many of the others.

Jesus loved, respected, and relied upon Judas. He chose Judas. He was a very smart man and had great talent and a good heart. But what is he remembered for? His weakness!

Remember, just like Peter, James, and John, this man had given up a lot to follow Christ. He believed in the message, and it was Judas's **greatest desire** to follow after Christ and be in the ministry.

But as you know, Judas had a weakness—money. Jesus knew this and yet He gave the man an opportunity to use his talent in the area of finances. What always amazes me about the relationship between Jesus and Judas was that while Jesus *knew* Judas was stealing money, He didn't tell anybody.

Jesus loved Judas so much that he extended grace and mercy to the man, when He knew he was stealing. Why? **Jesus loved Judas more than He loved the money in the bag.** So, Jesus was merciful toward Judas.

Some people think that Judas stole the whole time. I don't believe that. I think that he didn't start out stealing because he believed in the cause—he loved the ministry. But somewhere along the way, his love of money overcame his love of the ministry. This is something you never want to happen to you, whether you're in ministry or in business.

DON'T REST ON YOUR RICHES

When you see some success, don't let it change you. Don't start thinking that money is going to always save you or that it doesn't matter anymore that you are focused on thinking good and determined thoughts.

Mental maps still matter, I don't care if you've already reached your goal or not. Dream another dream. Move forward. There is always somewhere higher for you to go. It may be in a different area of life, but you're not built to stay stagnant. Until the day you die, you want to be moving forward . . . even if your goal becomes to just rock on the porch and pour your love and wisdom into your grandkids or the kids next door. God is never finished with you.

But, if you're in your earning years and you've made a success of your life financially, don't sit back and trust in your riches, thinking that you don't need to seek after God anymore. Proverbs 11:28 says that, *"He that trusteth in his riches shall fall: but the righteous shall flourish as a branch."*

Trust should be reserved for God and people, not inanimate things like money.

Proverbs 23:5 says, *"Wilt thou set thine eyes upon that which is not? for riches certainly make themselves wings; they fly away as an eagle toward heaven."* In other words, money can fly away! I don't care if you are a billionaire, you can be penniless in a moment. Remember the Great Depression in America? If you don't think the economy can collapse again, you're living in a dream world. Anything can happen, so you can't trust in your money.

Judas didn't understand this. Judas began to twist, and like all thieves, I believe he began to make excuses and justify his actions—which is where the next lesson in this book is going. Are you ready? Let's look at the life of Judas and how you can learn from his weakness.

THE LAST SUPPER . . . WHO'S NEXT TO JESUS?

Judas was a great disciple of Christ at one time. Then his love of money started twisting his thoughts. He lost focus. Maybe Judas's thievery started on one of those errands Jesus was always sending him to do . . . you know, like giving alms, or money, to the poor. Jesus was a great giver.

When Judas left the table at the Last Supper, the disciples just assumed he was going to give alms to the poor. Why would they assume that, if it wasn't commonplace?

Jesus gave everybody a heads-up at the Last Supper about His betrayer.

I mean, have you ever wondered how Judas could "dip the bread in the cup" like Jesus said the betrayer would do, and *not* be seen by the others . . . unless they were sitting pretty close to one another at the supper?

People think the old paintings of Christ and the Last Supper are just like photographs, as if da Vinci had a camera at the Last Supper and said, "Okay, now, everybody, listen up! Stand on that side of the table so I can get a good shot! Judas, come on, look a little angry, would you?!" That's a joke, but you get the point. The best way to know this kind of thing is by reading the Bible and looking into what was common in that day.

History tells us that, unlike the famous painting, the Last Supper would have most likely been eaten at a table shaped like a U with Jesus on the far end and Judas being the one most likely sitting right beside Him. This is how the Jews of that time would have sat at a large gathering. The person of most prominence wouldn't have been in the middle, but on the end.

Here's what I think. Because Judas handled the ministry finances, he was called upon regularly by Jesus to pay for the rooms, the meals, and the boat rides, etcetera. I believe that Jesus would have been talking to Judas often. I think that Jesus would send him to give money and even thank the others for giving to the work a lot.

It's obvious Judas paid for many meals, like the Last Supper. Common sense says that it wouldn't have been called the "last" if there hadn't been any before! I believe that Judas sat right next to Jesus so that Jesus could give him direction easily.

After all, Jesus was so quiet about how He gave; He would not have shouted out across the table, "Hey! Judas! You guys, be quiet, I'm trying to talk to Judas! Psst! You remember that poor woman we saw today? I want you to go and find her and give her a hundred bucks . . . hey, do you hear me, Judas?!"

No, the Bible tells us that Jesus didn't even want His other *hand* to be aware of a gift. So, do you think He'd want the whole room to know the details of his giving?

When Jesus said, *"Verily, verily, I say unto you, that one of you shall betray Me"* during the Last Supper, it was an announcement that freaked everybody out (John 13:21). Immediately each person started wondering about himself and asking Jesus who would do it.

Jesus's response was, *"'It is he to whom I shall give a piece of bread when I have dipped* it'"* (John 13:26, NKJV). Yet, no disciple saw the bread dipped in the dish and no disciple saw Christ give Judas the bread—not one!

Why didn't anybody see the dipping going on? Because Judas was right next to Jesus.

If Judas was way on the other side, everyone else at that Last Supper would have seen what happened . . . and they would have killed Judas before he had a chance to run out the door! Peter would have knocked that boy silly!

But Jesus didn't have to yell or reach down and dip . . . because, I believe, Jesus was sitting very close to Judas.

JUDAS'S REJECTION OF CHRIST

". . . And having dipped the bread, He gave it *to Judas Iscariot,* the son *of Simon. Now after the piece of bread, Satan entered him. Then Jesus said to him, 'What you do, do quickly'"* (John 13:26–27, NKJV).

At that moment, Satan entered Judas and Jesus spoke both to Judas and to the spirit motivating him and said, "What you do, do quickly."

Now, I want you to notice something here: Satan was not *in* Judas before that moment of confrontation. Before this moment, Judas was toying with the mercy and grace of God. He was playing games and stealing, thinking that he was untouchable . . . which was a great mistake.

But there came a moment, and it happened at this final supper, that Judas's playing caught up with him. I want you to notice that, at the very moment when Jesus confronted Judas about his betrayal, a change occurred in Judas. I believe that suddenly, Judas knew for certain that Jesus was aware of his betrayal . . . and he didn't care.

Judas still could have repented. He could have turned down the bread and said, "Jesus, forgive me." He could have scrapped his plans of betrayal right then and there, but Judas didn't do that. Instead, Judas made a choice to completely reject Jesus Christ.

He took the bread, a symbol of his betrayal, from Jesus's hand and, at that moment, Judas's decision gave Jesus's adversary, Satan, a way to gain full entrance into his life. Suddenly, the weakness—his love of money—that he was indulging in caused him to open up and be fully controlled by the devil.

Judas put the bread into his mouth, got up from the table, and left the room.

The lesson here is that Jesus knows what's going on in our lives. He is merciful, some would say, to a fault. If I was Jesus, I would have slapped that boy silly! Jesus didn't do that. He was merciful, giving Judas a chance to turn things around. He's going to give you mercy, too, but if you decide to keep doing what you know is wrong, one day it's going to come back to bite you. Nobody sows something like that without reaping it!

JUDAS, ARE YOU GOING TO GIVE ALMS?

What did the disciples say when Judas walked out of the room? Did they say, "There's the betrayer! Knock him to the ground!" No. Did they say, "Oh, Judas must be going to the bathroom." No. Did they say, "Judas is going pay the bill." No, they didn't assume that, as the one with the money, Judas was going to pay for the meal either.

The Bible tells us in John 13:29, *"For some of them thought, because Judas had the bag, that Jesus had said unto him, Buy those things that we have need of against the feast; or, that he should give something to the poor."*

Why would they assume that Judas was maybe giving money to the poor? Because he'd probably done it a thousand times before. I wonder how many times the disciples saw Jesus tell Judas to get up, go and bless someone with money? I wonder how many times they heard Jesus say, "Judas, do you remember that lady we saw today? I want you to go and bless her with X amount right now."

Judas moved when Jesus spoke. The disciples saw that. I believe that it was probably on one of those trips to give alms to the poor that Judas began indulging in his greatest weakness.

How did the thievery start? Small, of course, like everything else. Most people don't sin big on the first try, they work up to it. It's human nature. That's why you have to nip a weakness in the bud before you get too used to doing it. The more you do something you know you shouldn't, the easier it is to go further into it the next time. Eventually it has a hold on you and will control you . . . and nothing should control you. Don't give your power away. Don't give in to a weakness. Otherwise, what happened to Judas might happen to you.

Could Jesus have told him to give one amount and Judas given a smaller amount and pocketed the difference? Sure! It would have been one way to steal without anyone knowing, except Jesus, of course. And, like any other person indulging in his weakness, Judas justified his actions. It's the only way he could continue in the ministry and still do wrong day in and day out.

I used to wonder how preachers could do just terrible things and then get back in the pulpit and preach. I used to wonder, *How can a man go and sin with a hooker one minute and get behind the pulpit and preach the next? What? Does he ask Jesus, "Hey, Jesus, would you mind stepping out in the hall? I've got some lusting to take care of here."* I just couldn't get my mind around it, the sheer lack of integrity.

Then, one day, it dawned on me . . . they've conditioned their mind to justify sin. Sad, but true. They're anointed, but weak, and they indulge little by little, until they do what they thought they'd never do. I think Judas was the same way.

Judas had been conditioning his mind to justify stealing from Jesus's ministry. I believe that it is very probable that Judas told himself things like . . . *the poor have nothing anyway and even if I give them less than what Jesus had said, they're still getting blessed . . . aren't they?*

Watch out for this kind of thinking in your own life! When you justify sin, you're treading in "Judas territory." You are wading around in self-deception. And, like Judas, you're only robbing yourself. That sin is going to rob you blind.

NO ONE IS UNTOUCHABLE

Judas thought he was untouchable. While he definitely had a weakness for money, I think that his greatest weakness was assuming that, because he worked for the Son of God, nothing bad could really come to him.

Judas knew the nature of Christ. He saw that Jesus was extremely forgiving. He heard the sermons and saw the miracles. He knew that Jesus was powerful. But He also saw that even the worst in society were forgiven of their sin.

Judas also noticed that every time somebody or something tried to attack or kill Jesus, the attempt was unsuccessful.

He also knew Jesus's history. Judas knew that Jesus had been saved from harm since He was a little baby. Remember, Herod wanted Jesus dead when He was an infant. It didn't happen.

Judas was also on the boat the day the wind and waves kicked up, but he saw that the storm couldn't break up Jesus's boat. He'd just tell the wind to quit and it would quit!

So, at the time of the Last Supper, Judas knew that the Pharisees wanted Jesus dead. But he probably thought that wouldn't happen either. Nothing else had harmed Jesus, why would the Pharisees be any different?

Judas saw that the Pharisees couldn't *really* harm Jesus before. He saw that they tried to push Jesus off of a cliff, but Jesus just walked away. No struggles. They tried to catch Him by testing his knowledge and interpretation of the Law, but they could not find any fault in His answers. Jesus was wise and He not only always walked away from their violence, but He outwitted them all in mere conversation.

So, I believe that Judas thought everything would always be okay.

Jesus and His ministry would continue on just as it had for the last few years, regardless of what he did.

But for some reason, Judas needed those thirty pieces of silver bad! Bad enough to justify betraying Jesus. After all, he may have assumed that, if caught, Jesus would just forgive him, and since the soldiers couldn't hurt Jesus anyway, what difference would his betrayal really make?

This is the kind of justification that I believe went on with Judas. I think he convinced himself that if he could only get the money, everything else would work out. He convinced himself that he was untouchable.

Don't ever think that you are untouchable. I don't care who you work for! Your boss might be the Son of God, but you can still burn in Hell. I don't care how much money you've got. You can still lose it. And I don't care how merciful you think your wife is, either. You run around on that woman enough and you might find yourself eating beans out of a can, sitting alone in an empty house with half of your money in the bank!

Sin happens. The tide turns. And, there's a point when a man goes one step too far in the wrong direction. David took the woman. Judas took the bread . . . and the money! What are you taking? Remember, it *all* starts in the mind—the place where mental maps are formed, maps that will take you somewhere, either good or bad. Stop the weakness before it leads you off the straight and narrow road. Your best life is on the straight and narrow.

PRESSURE AND THIRTY LOUSY PIECES OF SILVER

Desperation. It's what I think caused Judas to betray Christ. I think he felt pressured and felt that he *had* to have those thirty pieces of silver.

Why would a man betray God for thirty pieces of silver from others when he'd already been getting what he wanted straight out of the ministry bag? Why wouldn't he just steal from the next poor person that Jesus told him to go and give alms to? Wouldn't that have been easier?

It's called pressure! Pressure to have something will make a man act in desperation. I call it the "spirit of stupid." It jumps on people all the time. That's a joke, of course, but Judas's situation was nothing to laugh about. This boy got himself into a situation. I believe that something happened and he felt pressured to have that silver, no matter what.

What makes a man do irrational things for the love of money? Sometimes it is sheer greed. Most times, it is because pressure is being applied somewhere or somehow. Like a gambler in debt to the wrong people, a man in financial pressure will sweat it, get irritated, and act irrationally.

Why did Judas need the money so bad? Maybe he feared being exposed as a thief. Maybe an audit time was coming and he had to replace silver and balance that bag, or else he was going to be found out. Sure, it could have been something else. We may never know until we get to Heaven but, whatever the case, it's obvious to me that there was great pressure on Judas to get that silver . . . at any cost.

The Bible is filled with teachings about human nature that can give you an edge in life. You don't have to learn everything by experience. You don't have to fall in a ditch to know it's dirty. That's why God gave us His Word.

Sure, some direction in the Bible is plain "do this and you'll prosper" type of instruction. But a lot of direction comes in the form of life stories, like this one. Through Judas, we learn that unrestrained weakness and rationalizing sin can not only steer you off course in your life, but it can destroy your life. Judas's story is just filled with lessons!

SNAP! JUDAS'S BREAKING POINT

What was the breaking point? What drove Judas to betray Jesus? It was a woman! A woman with a precious and expensive gift for Jesus. Her name was Mary, and when she broke that alabaster box of ointment and poured it on Jesus's feet in John 12:5, it was Judas who got angry and spat, *"Why was not this ointment sold for three hundred pence, and given to the poor?"*

The Bible tells us, *"This he said, not that he cared for the poor; but because he was a thief, and had the bag, and bare what was put therein"* (John 12:6).

Judas wanted that money! He was ticked off that it was "wasted" on Jesus's feet . . . yet Mark 14:9 records Jesus as saying this about Mary's gift, *"Verily I say unto you, Wheresoever this Gospel shall be preached throughout the whole world, this also that she hath done shall be spoken of for a memorial of her."*

Whew! Jesus not only told Judas that she had done right, but made the proclamations that her precious gift would be spoken of throughout the world. Now, this made Judas hot—this is the very first time we read about Jesus putting Judas in his place, and Judas didn't like it one bit.

Jesus would not let Judas steal from Him this time. Jesus had enough. He knew that He was headed to the cross. He knew that Mary's ointment was part of His burial ritual, and Jesus would not let her great gift be stolen.

The Bible says that right after this, Judas was filled with indignation and went straightaway to make a deal with the priest to betray Jesus. Snap! That was his breaking point! He was not only a thief but prideful. He didn't like being put in his place.

I believe that because of his desperation for the money, and the threat of being exposed, and the humiliation of being stopped by Christ, Judas lost all rational thought. He snapped and went on straightaway to betray Christ.

There is a great lesson in Judas's reaction to being stopped that we can learn from. Have you ever seen someone who thinks he can do anything and never be stopped suddenly get a reality check?

Judas got a reality check but, because his heart was so hard and cold, it didn't cause him to see the error of his ways and repent. It caused him to get angry and betray.

So, you know that, if you are corrected by someone else and you get angry about it enough to want to hurt that person, you're in the same frame of mind as Judas. Remember that. Let it sink in, because this is a lesson that can help you to stop your emotions from driving you to do something you'll later regret.

Human emotion gets involved, but our spirit should prevail. It doesn't always, I know. But there should be a time when we ask ourselves, *What do I want? Do I want to go this way? Or do I want to go that way?* In other words, *Do I want to build a mental map to a good destiny or do I want to go the other way?*

Judas chose to go the wrong way.

"I AM HE!"

The night Jesus was betrayed, it was Judas who was leading the pack. He was walking toward Jesus and a crowd of soldiers sent by the Pharisees followed behind him. When Judas saw Jesus, he immediately greeted Him with a kiss . . . a secret signal to the soldiers.

Jesus looked at His close disciple, and in Luke 22:48 it records Jesus as saying this: *"Judas, betrayest thou the Son of man with a kiss?"* In other words, "You betray me with a sign of affection? After all the mercy and grace I've extended to you, Judas? This is what you do?"

Judas was shocked. The Bible says he backed up, which tells us that he didn't expect that kind of reaction from Jesus and that he was suddenly afraid.

Just then, a band of men and officers from the chief priests and Pharisees came up behind Judas with lanterns and torches and weapons. Jesus knew what was going on, and He didn't run away. Instead, He spoke to them first. He confronted them with a question, "Whom seek ye?" And they answered, "Jesus of Nazareth!" (John 18:4–5).

Jesus looked at them and said, **"I am He,"** and as soon as Jesus spoke those words, the Scripture says that everybody in that band of men fell to the ground! That's right! The power of the Son of God releasing Himself caused them to fall on their faces, on the ground! (John 18:6) Power hit them and torches fell all over the place!

Judas probably looked at that and thought, *See, we ain't got a problem. We're going to be outta here, just like we've been doing for the last three years. We're going to be in Capernium in the next couple of hours anyway, and then I'm going to tell Him I took some money from Him and He's going to forgive me . . . and it'll be all right.*

But Jesus did something that Judas never thought He would do. He didn't walk away. He didn't leave the soldiers on the ground. No, He stood right where He was. He allowed the soldiers to get up. Then He asked them one more time who they sought and released Himself into the hands of those men.

Jesus had made His decision. It was His time and, although He had prayed all that night in the garden of Gethsemane to let the cup pass, He knew then that the cup would not pass from His lips. God's will had to be done and Jesus knew it . . . He was going to the cross.

DEATH-GRIP GRIEF

Now, in Judas's mind, what was happening was unthinkable. *No!* Judas thought, *They can't kill You! Let's get out of here! Jesus, what are You doing?!* But Jesus walked off with those men . . . and it was at that very moment that, I believe, Judas fully realized the magnitude of what he had done. *He* had been the betrayer. *He* had been the one prophesied in the Old Testament. *He* had sent his beloved Master to the cross.

Suddenly, Judas really *knew* what he'd done. At that moment, there was no more justification in his mind. There was no more deception. The light was bright on his betrayal and it was clear to him that he had just done the unthinkable.

The guilt was overwhelming to Judas. It swirled around his mind and grieved his soul so much that, when he realized that Jesus was condemned to death, the Bible says he went out and hanged himself.

Then Judas, which had betrayed him, when he saw that
He was condemned, repented himself, and brought again
the thirty pieces of silver to the chief priests and elders,
Saying, I have sinned in that I have betrayed the innocent
blood. And they said, What is that to us? see thou to that.
And he cast down the pieces of silver in the temple,
and departed, and went and hanged himself.
MATTHEW 27:3–5

Judas could not face living another moment with the full knowledge of what he'd done. Guilt consumed this man to the point of self-destruction.

Judas lost it all. His greatest weakness caused him to betray the one he loved. It stopped his greatest desire, to be a true disciple of Jesus Christ, from coming to pass . . . it stole his original "mental map" which was supposed to lead him down the path of true discipleship, and steered him off-course onto a thief and betrayer's course. Never forget Judas.

REMEMBER JUDAS, AND THEN BE LIKE PETER!

Remember Judas when you consider indulging in a weakness that you know has no good end. Remember Judas when you want to deny your sin. Remember Judas when you're tempted to make excuses. Remember Judas!

There is a real devil out there who wants to lead you down the wrong path. God will not force your hand to do right. He will be merciful with you. He will love you, even if you steal right out from under His nose.

But, don't think that you can keep on sinning against God and get away with it. The Bible tells us that *"For the wages of sin is death . . ."* which simply means that if you continue going on the wrong path, you'll end up in the wrong place, *". . . but the gift of God is eternal life through Jesus Christ our Lord"* (Romans 6:23).

Don't allow an unfit desire to blind your eyes. Sin is reality. It's "missing the mark" and going off course. Face yourself now. Don't create a past that will hinder your future . . . because the past never sees the future. God forgives, but people never forget and it's hard to do big things when people don't trust you anymore.

God can help you to strengthen that area in your life now so that it doesn't rob you of your good future. And if you hit the end of your rope, if you think you've done all that can be done and that there is no forgiveness for you, remember Peter.

Remember, the only difference between Peter and Judas was that Judas couldn't forgive himself and wouldn't ask for forgiveness from God. Peter denied Christ, and that was a betrayal, too—he denied Christ three times, three! He didn't do any better than Judas in that respect.

Yet, unlike Judas who could not receive forgiveness for what he'd done, Peter didn't deny the amazing grace of God. Peter did not deny the forgiving power of Christ. He knew that, no matter what, the Lord was able to cleanse him from his betrayal and help him back on the right road in his life.

Peter didn't run away from mercy. Instead, He ran into mercy and in Matthew 16:18, Jesus said, *Thou art Peter, and upon this rock I will build My church; and the gates of Hell shall not prevail against it!"*

Was Peter's destiny impossible? Yes! It was impossible for a man who denied God to lead the Church of God and defy the gates of Hell. It was impossible with man, but it was totally possible with God!

There is nothing that God can't turn around, no life that He can't make great. He would have forgiven even Judas had Judas given Him the opportunity. How much more will He forgive you?

FREE WILL AND GOOD CHOICES

You are God's beloved. You have a place in His heart, no matter what you've done and no matter how great your weakness seems. You have a place at His table and His arms of love are open to you now. There is nothing that you've done that is "too bad" for the saving grace of God. He will forgive you, but you have to make the choice to turn to Him.

Making the right choices in your thoughts help you to build good mental maps—foundations of good thoughts that will lead you to make the right choices in life. You can't reach a good, divinely ordered destiny if you make willful, wrong choices. What you do out of ignorance is one thing, but what you do when you know better is another thing entirely!

You see, God respects the free will He gave each of us. He respects your right to choose a good destiny in Him, to build positive mental maps that will lead you to positive ideas and positive actions. But He will also respect your right to choose negatively, to choose thoughts, ideas, and actions that lead to death, Hell, and the grave. Jesus has beaten those things at the cross, to make a way for you . . . but He will not force your hand or your heart to go the right way—His way, the forgiving way.

If you don't know Jesus as your Savior, stop right now and pray to Him. You can't walk a divine path without having the divine One living inside of you. All you have to do is just repent. Be humble. Receive His mercy, because it is there for you. Christ went to the cross for you. And He will forgive you of all your sin the moment you turn your heart to Him. Confess that you've gone the wrong way. Confess that He is the right way. Then, ask Him to come into your life and help you to start living right, to start building a good and determined thought-life, to start walking down the road to His divine destiny for you—which is His good plan for your life.

If you are already a believer, but you have been struggling and toying with a "greatest weakness" like David or Judas—something that you just haven't let go—stop right now and pray to God. Release that weakness to Him now. Rededicate your life to Him. Then, every day, make getting stronger in this area part of your mental map. Let your thoughts begin each morning with determination to love God, to live for God, and to enforce your decision to become strong in that area.

MORNING-BY-MORNING PRAYER

Do it in the morning. Just pray to God in your own way. Don't worry about sounding good. You can do it while you're still in bed, before you even get up. Or you can do it while you're brushing your teeth, or in the shower. Whether you pray out loud or to yourself is your choice. I choose to do it both ways.

You see, I'm a preacher. This is my life. Yet, I know that I haven't "arrived." Every day I must pray. Every day I must follow Christ. It is a reinforcement of my "general" mental map that keeps me going in the right direction.

If I let my flesh have its way, it would take me down the wrong path. So, I have to commit myself to God. I have to cast down the thoughts that want to steal God's good way from my life. I have to stop and think, and not act, on ideas that I know won't lead to anything good. These are decisions. They're like prayers. They facilitate my mental map—the determined thoughts I have about what I'm doing in my life and who I'm becoming along the way—and they keep me on God's good path for my life.

I've seen what David's weakness can do to a ministry. I've seen what Judas's weakness can do, too. And I don't want any part of it. You see, I have a destiny to fulfill. I could forfeit it for women or money, but I won't. I don't want to. It's my choice to create my own good life within the confines of God's will.

You have to get to that point where you are repulsed by the very thing that you are weak in . . . when you can look at what others have done with the same weakness and say, "No, I am not going that way." It's a decision to be holy, a decision to do right, a decision to ask for forgiveness when you need it, but to ultimately make Jesus your example and Jesus's way of doing things your goal in life.

That is the "big picture," because you may be only one person in the Body of Christ, but your life makes a difference. You're part of something bigger. What you think, what you say, and what you do matters to the Lord because it is going to affect your life, which in turn affects others as well. As believers we're part of the body of Christ—the Church of the Lord Jesus—and it's a Church that Christ says He will come back for one day.

Will we be ready? Will we have a list of regrets? Will we stand before Jesus and say, "Well, I could have done this . . . but I didn't" or "I should have done this, but I didn't"—No way! I don't know about you, but I don't want to have regrets. I don't want to have to need too much of the blood to wash away sin that I could have prevented. I don't want to frustrate the grace of God! I want to be a blessing to God and to others! I want to make the right choices and live out my mental map, day by day, until Jesus comes back—a life without regrets! This life is but a vapor, James 4:14 says, but it is a vapor that can be glory-filled!

So, will temptation come? Yes! That's the way life is. It came to Jesus, so you can bet it's coming to you. When it does, remember the lessons of David's and Judas's indulged weaknesses. Then remember Jesus! Remember His power! Remember His strength! He went to the cross for you. He made a way so that you can be free from that weakness junk, if you want to. You aren't alone. God will help you if you start relying on Him about it.

YOU AREN'T DESTINED TO BE WEAK!

The bottom line is that you can't do some things in your own strength. Willpower is not enough. You need God's power, living on the inside of you, to come out when you need it, which is why you need more of Him. Read the Word. Let it seep into you. It's going to clean up your mind and help you to get strong *inside* so that what happens *outside* won't affect you as much.

That power inside of you? It's up to you to let it out. Take ownership of it. Recognize it. If God is powerful and He lives in you, that makes you powerful even if you feel weak. It's a spiritual power that can come up and help you to conquer mental weakness.

Remember, you are not destined to be weak. That weakness is not from God, so it's no good. What's from God is always good. Call on Him. Ask Him for help. You can conquer any weakness, no matter what it is, if you commit to God and focus on becoming free of it. It can actually become a strength.

Morning by morning, choose God's path. He'll help you to stay on track so that you can fulfill His good plan for your life, and so that you can have and enjoy your "greatest desire." Who knows what that is? Who knows what it will be? But if you stick it out, God is going to help you to not only build a great mental map and not only begin walking on the best path for your life, but He's also going to help you to *stay* on that right way!

> *Enter ye in at the strait gate: for wide is the gate, and broad is the way, that leadeth to destruction, and many there be which go in thereat:*
> *Because strait is the gate, and narrow is the way, which leadeth unto life, and few there be that find it.*
> MATTHEW 7:13–14

Anybody can give up. Anybody can follow a weakness to the end. Be one of the few who find the narrow and always-rewarding path of God! This is only the way that leads to a truly good life!

CHAPTER 18

YOU ARE UNIQUE

THE FIRST MEETING I ever preached was in a cow pasture in Ladonia, Texas. It was a meeting they called a Brush Arbor Revival, where they'd laid down a bunch of sticks and put chicken wire on top. Then, they layered grass and tree limbs—sort of like a backwoods stage.

I looked out onto that makeshift stage and asked the man who was driving me around, "What if it rains?" There was no roof to speak of.

"Well," he said, "you'll get wet."

I said, "Oh, well, praise God, okay!"

I looked out over the pasture and saw cows grazing. When I asked the man if they were going to round up the cows for the night, he said they weren't doing it. It was the deal they'd cut with the guy who owned the land. They could use it, but the cows had to stay.

"Well, suppose the cows come in when I'm preaching," I asked.

"Oh, they won't come in," he said. "They don't like people."

Well, that night, I was preaching my first sermon in a cow pasture. I was preaching the best I could. My sermon was on Lazarus and people were snickering as I spoke. I didn't like it. Twenty minutes later, I started winding it up. People were laughing and some were looking at their watches, and I figured they'd had just about enough of this old Cajun boy.

So, I gave the altar call, my very first. I figured that even if my sermon wasn't so good, the Word alone would cause people to come and give their hearts to Jesus. So, I said, "Everybody, bow your heads and close your eyes." I was so excited that God was using me.

"Nobody look around. If you don't know Jesus tonight and you'd like to meet Him, I'm going to ask you right now, with every head bowed and every eye closed, to come up here and make Jesus the Lord of your life."

My eyes were closed tightly. I was intensely waiting for people to come forward—but no one came. Not one person.

"Mooooooooo!"

I heard the groan and my neck shot up quick. My eyes popped open and the new convert that stood before me had four legs. It was a moaning and groaning cow, right up front at the altar! People started laughing. But to me, it was not funny at all. I wanted to quit my calling right then and there.

The next week, they butchered the cow. I guess she needed to get her life straight before she met her Maker.

But that night, after the service, I was in bed and feeling like such a failure. I felt like my Cajun accent was a hindrance to my calling. I felt like nobody took me seriously, and I really wanted to be taken seriously.

What had happened to me? I'd found that my destiny as a minister of the Gospel wasn't exactly as I'd hoped it would be—it was different, it wasn't like that of the other preachers I'd admired. It was uniquely my own.

YOU ARE UNIQUE

The destiny I began to fulfill in the pulpit wasn't someone else's that I'd borrowed and tried on for size. It wasn't a suit with sleeves that were too long and trousers that were too short. For the ministry that God called me to, it was a suit that fit me perfectly. It may have been a different color than I'd thought I'd get, but it was mine and, soon enough, I came to terms with it and accepted it as my own.

God has given you a divine destiny, and it's not going to be like anyone else's destiny. It's your suit, your dress, your life! No matter what God calls you to do, He will use you in a unique way. Why? Because you are unique. You have something in you that is different from others.

God doesn't make clones. Even identical twins that look exactly alike on the outside have unique features on the inside. They may think alike, but not exactly alike. Why? Because we are all different— and it is good!

As a preacher, I am unique. God is using me to help others know more about Him, in my own way. Sometimes I'm funny, sometimes I'm deep, but I'm always me.

You're going to be the same way. If your heart is in the right place and you are simply "you," God is going to cause your uniqueness to shine. Your destiny will not be a carbon copy of someone else's, even of someone you admire. If you follow God, you're going to see that your destiny is uniquely your own.

IS IT EVERYONE'S DESTINY TO LIVE FOR GOD?

This is a question that comes up from time to time and the answer is yes. Yes! Each of us has been given the opportunity to either walk in our divine destiny and follow God or reject our divine destiny and go our own way. Shakespeare's Hamlet said, "To be or not to be, that is the question!" But the question really is, "To believe or not to believe." That determines what you'll be.

Before a person gets saved, he has the choice to either believe or not believe. His choice determines what he'll do in life.

The Word tells us that we are predestined to conform to the image of Christ Jesus—it's the destiny God has given us all. Yet, not everybody gets saved. Why? We live by choice and not by chance!

Fate is not a part of a believer's life. We are in control of our own spirituality. We have a great gift called free will. So, the choices we make as we move through our life will either propel us *toward* God or *away* from God, and each choice affects our life.

I believe with all my being that your divine destiny is to stick with God—from the moment you receive Him as your Savior to the moment you breathe your last breath. It's also your divine destiny to become the person He has created you to be.

Spiritually, physically, and financially, God wants the best for your life. And your personal best is always going to be found as you follow after God with a pure heart—wherever that road may lead you.

No one's destiny is to live for the devil. Even the devil had a choice to either follow after God or rebel against Him. He chose rebellion and damnation. However, because he had no tempter, he is eternally damned. Think about it. There was no one to tempt Satan. He drew up iniquity from his own being. He chose it out of vanity and a budding lust for glory. Yet, you and I—mankind—have not done this. We were lured away from God by the devil; we did not do it on our own.

God sent Jesus to save us from ourselves; to give us back what we lost in the Garden.

> For God so loved the world, that He gave His only begotten Son, that whosoever believeth in Him should not perish, but have everlasting life.
>
> For God sent not His Son into the world to condemn the world; but that the world through Him might be saved.
>
> He that believeth on Him is not condemned: but He that believeth not is condemned already, because He hath not believed in the name of the only begotten Son of God.
>
> And this is the condemnation, that light is come into

*the world, and men loved darkness rather than light,
because their deeds were evil.*

*For every one that doeth evil hateth the light, neither
cometh to the light, lest his deeds should be reproved.*

*But he that doeth truth cometh to the light, that his deeds
may be made manifest, that they are wrought in God.*

JOHN 3:16–21

WHEN LIGHT AND DARK COLLIDE

When it comes to salvation or anything else in life, we have choices.
In reality, there is only one good choice—salvation and following
after God.

As the Scripture above says, condemnation is already present on
this sin-sick planet. Yet, God loved us enough to send His Son, Jesus,
to pay the price so that we might be saved; so that the condemnation
of sin might be lifted from us.

Jesus *is* the light that came into the world. But some people love
darkness rather than light because they prefer evil. They don't want to
give up how they're living, and so they resent the light of the world.

The sin nature is at odds against Jesus and His nature. This is why
you see some people who are unsaved who literally hate the Gospel
and all it stands for. They loathe people who serve Jesus. What's happened to them? They've just gotten further along in the sin nature.
They've saturated themselves with darkness to the point that they
hate the light.

When you choose to walk in your divine destiny and follow after
Christ, get ready for some heat. Don't let it shock you when you are
persecuted for the Word's sake. It's not about you, it's about Jesus.
It's about light and darkness colliding. Those people might not even
realize it, but they are living under the curse of sin and it has affected
them to the core. The bright light that shines within you is a threat to
their thinly veiled darkness.

John 3:21 tells us that, when we come into the light, our deeds or actions will start to *manifest* God's goodness—and those deeds are known by everyone to be wrought, or created, in God. Isn't that amazing?

Galatians 5:22–23 puts it best when it says, *"But the fruit of the Spirit is love, joy, peace, longsuffering, gentleness, goodness, faith, meekness, temperance: **against such there is no law**."*

There is no law against the fruit of the Spirit. Goodness is part of the Christian life and it's recognized as godly.

NOBODY IS HOPELESS

Sure, there are people who do good deeds and yet are not saved. But they are acting on the goodness of God. They may not have accepted Christ, but they have, somewhere along the line, accepted the idea that it's a good thing to do what's right. They know what is right and have not refused goodness.

You see, I believe that, without Satan's influence in this earth, all people would turn to Jesus. We were created for it. This is why we are so moved when we see someone acting selflessly toward another human being. When someone risks his life to save another, we call him a hero. When we see someone put another first, we are impressed. When we see a truly peaceful or joyful person, we are attracted to that person. Why? Because we were created to be that way, too. Our very being connects with and notices deeds that are wrought by God.

Sin came into the earth and warped man's viewpoint, but no one is so far gone that God can't help him. No one is beyond His reach. The blood of Jesus washes away all sin and iniquity. It shines a bright light in the darkness, revealing a way out.

Jesus births His bright light within a man and saves him from himself, glory! The light of the world, Jesus, helps us to start over in life and begin walking on the road to divine destiny. It helps us to make something of ourselves that we can be proud of!

THE LONGEST-RUNNING PLAY IN HISTORY

This life can be compared to the longest-running play in history. The scenes change and the people change, but each act continues to unfold as we move toward the final curtain in God's plan for man. Some people move toward their destiny in God, others move away from their destiny in God, but still, this story goes on and on.

If we choose to accept our destiny, if we choose to conform to the image of Christ Jesus, then we become the characters that God has hand-selected for this generation.

Take me for example. I'm not a funny man by nature. I wasn't a funny man before I gave my heart to Jesus. I was cold and determined, but I never cracked jokes unless I was on drugs! After I got saved, I didn't suddenly become funny in my personal life. No, I was on a quest to know more about God. I was bold. I was tenacious. But I wasn't funny.

What happened to me? Destiny! From the moment that I began to preach, people began to laugh. At first, I thought they were laughing at me. But I soon figured out that they were hearing a lighthearted side of the Gospel that ended up cutting them right in the heart. They'd start laughing at one of the stories from my own life, and then I'd hit them with a serious point! Unsaved people would suddenly get convicted and come to the altar and get saved. It was great!

It still is great! Why? Because I didn't fight my calling. There are times to be serious and times to laugh. Sometimes those spaces of time collide! That has often been my "suit" so to speak, and I don't try on any other minister's clothes. I know what fits me. I do what God calls me to do. In other words, I know that if the suit doesn't fit, it's not mine.

CHAPTER 19

IF THE SUIT DON'T FIT, IT'S NOT YOURS!

As a kid, I saw a lot of so-called Christians who said one thing and did another. They were living out their lives in other people's suits. They were acting one way and preaching another. I didn't like it when I was five years old, and I still don't like it today.

When we choose to follow after God, it is more than an emotional cry for help. It's a choice, a decision, to accept the blood of Jesus for the remission of our sins. It's a decision we make to put on our robe of righteousness.

The robe of righteousness that is available to us came at a high price. Salvation is free to us, but it definitely didn't come cheap. It cost Jesus His life.

As a child, I was raised in church. But, I didn't get saved at a young age even though I was raised around Christians. Why? Because I saw a lot of people walking around in suits that didn't fit.

At an early age, I chose to go the other way. It's not that I didn't believe in God, but I figured that, if He did exist, He was way "up there," and since He wasn't helping anybody "down here," why should I serve Him?

Nobody I saw seemed to be doing what he said and, as a child, I took that to mean that God wasn't doing what He said, either. I was wrong, and I found it out later in my life, but still, as a young boy, I decided to go my own way. I never wanted to be like the wishy-washy people I grew up around.

So, when I set out to sin, I was good at it. I didn't sin halfway. I was going to Hell with gusto! I was drinking booze for breakfast. I was snorting cocaine and taking pills for fun. I was playing rock music and living a life of women, wine, and song. The money was good, but after I'd acquired what I wanted, I realized that I was still empty inside.

As I mentioned earlier, I got saved in a bathroom in Boston, Massachusetts, after I heard the Gospel preached on TV. That day, my sin was washed away, and Jesus clothed me in a spiritual robe of righteousness.

Like Isaiah 61:10 says, I was full of joy knowing that God had clothed me with the garments of salvation and covered me with the robe of righteousness. I became part of the bride of Christ—decked out in Him!

After that day, I wasn't interested in playing church and getting my ears tickled with a nice and sweet sermon. I decided that, if I was going to be a Christian, I didn't want to do it halfway. I wanted to walk tall in my garment of salvation! I wanted to strut in my robe of righteousness and show others that they could get one, too, glory to God!

I wanted to live what I heard preached every day. I wanted to live by faith in God and fulfill my own divine destiny!

DAVID GOT NO RESPECT!

A few chapters back, I shared about David and his greatest weakness, but there is another element to David's beginnings as a king that I want to share with you now.

Even though David had problems with lust, he was really a great man in many other respects. He was a man after God's own heart because he readily repented. He didn't always make excuses. He fell on his face and repented, got up, and tried to do right again. We can all relate to that!

David was unique in that he was a king at heart. But, remember, David didn't *look* like a king. He was a musician. He sang on the mountainside to his sheep. He was ruddy-faced, red-haired, and doe-eyed—but he had the heart of a king nevertheless.

When Samuel anointed David in obedience to God, nothing in David's outward appearance revealed the tenacity, loyalty, and the heart that was within him. Yet, God saw it and knew that his destiny, his *suit,* was that of a king.

Did anybody's opinion of David change after he was anointed? No. You see, people don't care how much fresh oil you've got. They don't care what other people say about you. You won't become a king in anyone's eyes until you do something to prove yourself kingly. David got no respect!

Now, I want you to remember that David was the youngest of all of Jesse's sons. He was considered so unworthy that his own father didn't bother to call him for the lineup. He was nothing like Moses, the great man of God who led Israel out of captivity in Egypt. Moses was the only man in the Bible that God talked with face to face.

Think about it: God never called Jesus the son of *Moses.* He called him the son of *David.* What greater honor could God bestow on a man? And, yet, no one saw David the way God saw him. They didn't honor him in any way and, most likely, his family told him, "Go on back to your sheep, boy. You're still nothing but a red-headed singing sheepherder." I'm paraphrasing, but you get the point! Notice that even *after* David was anointed king, he didn't get much more respect. The Bible doesn't record Jesse talking to his son much.

By 1 Samuel 17, a war is going on between the children of Israel and the Philistines. David's older brothers were in Saul's army and already on the front lines of battle.

Finally, Jesse called David to get involved. But it wasn't in the way you might think. Jesse wanted his youngest, anointed-to-be-king son, to do a food run! He said, and I'm paraphrasing again, "Your brothers need some food. Stop singing on the mountainside and get yourself to the battlefield with some cheese and bread."

TRASH-TALKING PHILISTINE

David had no way of knowing when he left home with a bunch of cheese that he was about to walk on stage for God. He had no idea that he was about to become the key player on the scene—that he was about to fulfill his destiny!

> Now the Philistines gathered their armies together to battle, and were gathered together at Sochoh, which belongs to Judah; they encamped between Sochoh and Azekah, in Ephes Dammim.
> And Saul and the men of Israel were gathered together, and they encamped in the Valley of Elah, and drew up in battle array against the Philistines.
> The Philistines stood on a mountain on one side, and Israel stood on a mountain on the other side, with a valley between them.
>
> 1 SAMUEL 17:1–3, NKJV

These weren't just two armies facing off; they were two kingdoms. One kingdom served Jehovah and the other served Dagon. Notice that Dagon always seemed to have better equipment and bigger people. The Philistines had a giant named Goliath as their champion. Goliath had a head as big as a microwave and a mouth to match. He was a trash-talking Philistine who made the Israelites tremble.

> Now Saul and they and all the men of Israel were in the Valley of Elah, fighting with the Philistines.
> So David rose early in the morning, left the sheep with

a keeper, and took the things and went as Jesse had com-manded him. And he came to the camp as the army was going out to the fight and shouting for the battle.

For Israel and the Philistines had drawn up in battle array, army against army.

And David left his supplies in the hand of the supply keeper, ran to the army, and came and greeted his brothers.

Then as he talked with them, there was the champion, the Philistine of Gath, Goliath by name, coming up from the armies of the Philistines; and he spoke according to the same words. So David heard them.

And all the men of Israel, when they saw the man, fled from him and were dreadfully afraid.

So the men of Israel said, "Have you seen this man who has come up? Surely he has come up to defy Israel; and it shall be that the man who kills him the king will enrich with great riches, will give him his daughter, and give his father's house exemption from taxes in Israel."

Then David spoke to the men who stood by him, saying, "What shall be done for the man who kills this Philistine and takes away the reproach from Israel? For who is this uncircumcised Philistine, that he should defy the armies of the living God?"

1 SAMUEL 17:19–26, NKJV

ELIAB'S JEALOUSY

I want you to notice what is coming out of David's mouth. The army of God had been terrified by Goliath's taunting. They hadn't even thought about God's covenant. David asked, *"For who is this uncir-cumcised Philistine, that he should defy the armies of the living God?"* (1 Samuel 17:26). That's covenant talk.

They told David that whoever killed Goliath would get a woman. You don't tell that to a seventeen-year-old boy without kicking up his hormones. David was excited, but Eliab's heart problem was finally revealed.

> *Now Eliab his oldest brother heard when he spoke to the men; and Eliab's anger was aroused against David, and he said, "Why did you come down here? And with whom have you left those few sheep in the wilderness? I know your pride and the insolence of your heart, for you have come down to see the battle."*
>
> *And David said, "What have I done now? Is there not a cause?"*
>
> 1 SAMUEL 17:28–29, NKJV

Eliab wouldn't give his brother a break. He didn't thank him for the cheese, and on top of that, he rode him about just being curious. Why? Because Eliab was jealous of David.

This is the same problem that crops up between friends, business associates, and even in many ministries. David loved Eliab. He wanted to please him. But Eliab was threatened by David and couldn't speak a kind word, much less be supportive. So, you can see how easy it was for David to be hurt and yet, he didn't let his brother steal his passion. He also didn't lose his anointing to be king just because he wasn't being treated like a king.

> *Now when the words which David spoke were heard, they reported them to Saul; and he sent for him.*
>
> *Then David said to Saul, "Let no man's heart fail because of him; your servant will go and fight with this Philistine."*
>
> 1 SAMUEL 17:31–32, NKJV

SAUL'S FEAR

David was willing to do whatever it took. Now, again, he didn't look the part, and Saul must have been looking at his red hair and thinking, *Listen to the punk kid flapping his lip. What does he know?*

David may have been young, but he knew enough to wonder why the king of Israel hadn't fought Goliath. The Bible says that Saul was head and shoulders taller than anyone in Israel. He looked the part. But the truth is that Saul didn't fight because Saul was afraid. He knew the presence of God had left him.

> And Saul said to David, "You are not able to go against this Philistine to fight with him; for you are a youth, and he a man of war from his youth."
>
> But David said to Saul, "Your servant used to keep his father's sheep, and when a lion or a bear came and took a lamb out of the flock, I went out after it and struck it, and delivered the lamb from its mouth; and when it arose against me, I caught it by its beard, and struck and killed it.
>
> "Your servant has killed both lion and bear; and this uncircumcised Philistine will be like one of them, seeing he has defied the armies of the living God."
>
> 1 SAMUEL 17:33–36, NKJV

PAST VICTORIES AND FUTURE CONFLICTS

David understood a powerful principle. **Past victories strengthen you for future conflicts.** David knew that he was a kid. He knew that he'd never been to war. But, he remembered that he had fought hard before . . . and won.

David not only remembered that God helped him kill the lion and the bear that threatened to eat his sheep, but he also made his past victory known to the right person at the right time. He wanted Saul to know that he was up for the battle.

> Moreover David said, "The LORD, who delivered me from the paw of the lion and from the paw of the bear, He

*will deliver me from the hand of this Philistine." And Saul
said to David, "Go, and the LORD be with you!"
So Saul clothed David with his armor, and he put a bronze
helmet on his head; he also clothed him with a coat of mail.*

1 SAMUEL 17:37–38, NKJV

Saul figured it was worth a shot, but he let David fight Goliath
on one condition: he had to wear Saul's armor. Do you realize what
Saul was trying to do? He was trying to make David look exactly like
Goliath because he believed that they had to be somewhat equal in
appearance in order for the battle to be won. Wrong!

Let me tell you something. You don't have to look like your enemy
to defeat him. You don't have to be tattooed from head to toe to reach
someone with a body full of tattoos. One big problem in the Body of
Christ is that we're all trying to look alike. Don't buy into that trap.
God made you an individual with unique gifts. You have a destiny
that is all your own, a suit that only you can fit!

David did a righteous thing. He submitted to authority. When
Saul told him to put on his suit of armor, David did it. Now, watch
what happened:

*David fastened his sword to his armor, and tried to
walk, for he had not tested them. And David said to Saul,
"I cannot walk with these, for I have not tested them." So
David took them off.*

1 SAMUEL 17:39, NKJV

LEARN WHEN TO TAKE THE WRONG SUIT OFF

David submitted to authority, but when he tried on the wrong suit
and saw that it didn't fit him, he knew enough to take the suit off.
Learn this lesson from David: *Always submit to authority, but never
submit to control.* In other words, if the suit doesn't fit, it's not yours! If

you happen to try on something for size, and it doesn't work, don't let it get to you. It's not for you. Your destiny isn't going to come packaged in somebody else's clothing.

Sure, I'd love to be a more theological, homiletical, and hermeneutical preacher, but God didn't call me to spend my life trying to attain "the perfect sermon." He didn't call me to be a man of eloquent speech. He called me to be who I am! He called me to preach and deliver His message to His people, not someone else's way but my own unique way. Together, we all make up the body of Christ and even people with the same gift—parts of the body—are going to showcase their gift a different way.

I love to hear very eloquent men speak the Word. I love to hear all the different accents—British, Australian, African, Chinese . . . whatever the accent, I enjoy the message! When I am in the company of great ministers of the Gospel, I refuse to get into the game of "one-upmanship" because God didn't make me any of those men. If I tried to be them, my suit wouldn't fit.

You see, in this life, God dressed us perfectly for the part we are to play. He created us with the inner qualities we need to do what He's called us to do. That's as true for you as it is for me.

KEEP YOUR ORIGINALITY

Do you know what made David a great king? He refused to wear the suit that didn't fit. He kept his individuality. He said, "I can't wear these! Thank you, Saul. They are beautiful clothes, but they aren't mine, and they don't fit. I've got a slingshot, and this guy has a head as big as a microwave. He's a target too big to miss."

> Then David said to the Philistine, "You come to me with a sword, with a spear, and with a javelin. But I come to you in the name of the LORD of hosts, the God of the armies of Israel, whom you have defied.
> "This day the LORD will deliver you into my hand, and

I will strike you and take your head from you. And this day
I will give the carcasses of the camp of the Philistines to
the birds of the air and the wild beasts of the earth, that
all the earth may know that there is a God in Israel.

"Then all this assembly shall know that the LORD does
not save with sword and spear; for the battle is the LORD's,
and He will give you into our hands."

So it was, when the Philistine arose and came and drew
near to meet David, that David hurried and ran toward the
army to meet the Philistine.

Then David put his hand in his bag and took out a
stone; and he slung it and struck the Philistine in his fore-
head, so that the stone sank into his forehead, and he fell
on his face to the earth.

So David prevailed over the Philistine with a sling and
a stone, and struck the Philistine and killed him. But there
was no sword in the hand of David.

Therefore David ran and stood over the Philistine, took
his sword and drew it out of its sheath and killed him, and
cut off his head with it. And when the Philistines saw that
their champion was dead, they fled.

1 SAMUEL 17:45–51, NKJV

David refused to wear what didn't fit him. He kept his originality. It was the right thing to do. He was at ease, in his own clothes and with his own weapon, and he was able to concentrate on doing his part in the battle.

THE BATTLE IS THE LORD'S

David killed the enemy that mocked God and proved himself kingly in the face of a fearful king. What made David a success? Not only did he keep his originality, but he also knew a very important thing: The battle is the Lord's. Many battles waged on earth are not God's.

They're the battles of men, spurred on by the evil influences of the devil.

Have your battles been overwhelming you? Let me ask you a few questions. Are you wearing somebody else's suit of armor? Does it fit? Are you struggling to do something that you were never meant to do? In other words, are you fighting someone else's battle? If so, God didn't give you the grace for it, and if He didn't, you're not going to be successful.

RISE TO THE OCCASION

Truthfully, Saul couldn't have fought David's battle. But as king, he must have been nervous. Here he was, giving part of the battle up to a ruddy-faced, teenage kid. Can you imagine him asking, "Um, David? What are you planning on doing to Goliath?"

"I'm gonna throw a rock at him."

Saul probably thought, *He's gonna make him madder!*

I can understand a little bit of how he felt, because I thought the same thing during an Oklahoma hailstorm. I was in Oklahoma with two minister friends when it happened. Now, I'm a Cajun from south Louisiana. I've been around hurricanes, but I've never heard hail hit a car like it hit the pickup we were sitting in. *Bam! Bam! Bam! Bam! Bam!* Jagged balls of ice fell like I'd never seen before. It was unbelievable!

The son of one of my minister friends was walking around with a shovel over his head and the hail just beat the fire out of that shovel. Eleven tornadoes hit the ground during that storm. All of a sudden, his daddy got a revelation. He stuck his finger out of the truck and said, "Devil! Stop it! I said, *Stop it!*"

I wanted to say, "Stop! You're making the storm madder! Leave it alone, we're in enough trouble!" I wanted out of that truck. But, you know, that hailstorm was nothing more than an opportunity to speak faith.

My friend understood what it meant to rise to the occasion. He knew that when God gives us an opportunity to do our part, we should never leave anything undone that might glorify Him. It glorified God for my friend to take authority over that hailstorm, just like it glorified God when David took authority over Goliath. It's going to glorify God when you rise to the occasion, too.

PURSUE YOUR DESTINY WITH PASSION

Remember, this life is a drama. It's a comedy. It's an action adventure that is going to go on until God says so. This life is filled with violence, sex, and envy because, let's face it, there's a Goliath around more than one corner.

Think about the part God has called you to play in this life. What is your destiny within the body of Christ? What will you do to bring glory to God? Do you have passion? Are you committed to your faith in God? David had passion, and he was committed to being a part of God's plan and defeating the enemy. He said, *"Is there not a cause?"* He knew that righteousness had to prevail. Do you?

David is a perfect example of a man with faith. He said to Saul, *"Let no man's heart fail because of him; your servant will go and fight with this Philistine"* (1 Samuel 17:32, NKJV).

That's the heart of a volunteer; the heart of the kind of man who goes to war without being asked, who cares enough about a cause to get behind it, even at great personal sacrifice. What a great destiny.

When I was a boy, I used to hear my dad and grandfather talk about the heroism of one such man. It was a terrible time in World War II when we were attacked so furiously by the Japanese. Men were dying in oil and grease at Pearl Harbor, Hawaii. Morale was low, and America was just entering the war. There didn't seem to be any way to strike back at Japan.

We needed something to rally us together.

Lt. Colonel Doolittle volunteered to lead an air strike against Japan. In the first "joint action" of the war, the Navy sailed Doolittle and the other volunteer pilots, along with their airplanes, as close as they could get to Japan. "Men, we may die," he said, knowing the cost of the cause. Taking off from the ship in waves so choppy they were washing over the deck, Doolittle flew into Japanese territory and struck an arrow into the heart of our enemy.

Like David's small stone hurling straight at Goliath's head, Doolittle made a crucial blow in the battle. There's nothing like the heart of a volunteer! There's nothing like a person who hears his cue from God and walks onstage at just the right moment in history.

YOU HAVE A UNIQUE DESTINY!

I don't have to know you to know that God has created a part for you in the greatest play on earth. It's a part that only *you* can play, a suit that only *you* can fit . . . and a divine destiny that only *you* can fulfill!

Forget about trying to fit someone else's mold. Keep your mental map free of those kinds of obstacles by accepting yourself and the utterly unique destiny that God has preordained for you!

Who knows? You may be the next king, the next hero of war, the next person who says, "I will be the one to stand up for righteousness. I will speak the truth and do what needs to be done. The battle isn't mine, it's the Lord's!"

CHAPTER 20

BLUE CORVETTE BLESSING

A FEW YEARS ago, I was preaching at a great church in Chicago, Illinois. A couple from the church picked up my wife and me from the airport, and we began the forty-minute drive to the church. We were all just talking and, as we came to a traffic light, I happened to glance out of my window. There, next to us, was a beautiful dark blue Corvette sports car.

"That's a gorgeous car," I whispered to Cathy. It just came out of my mouth. Now, I had not been thinking about cars at all, but I couldn't help noticing how beautiful that one was. I looked at Cathy and said, "I'll tell you what, if I ever got a Corvette, I'd like a blue one just like that, but I'd want a convertible, instead of a hardtop."

She said, "Jesse, do you want a 'vette? I can buy you a 'vette." Cathy is always looking for ways to bless me. She's a good wife!

I said, "No, I've always liked them, but, well, I've never thought about going out and buying one. You know, I've just always liked them." Cathy knows that I'm the kind of man who doesn't go out and buy every little thing I like. I just don't.

I looked over at that car and kept admiring it.

"That's a beautiful car," I said, "Whew, Lord, Cathy, I ought to go buy one so we can ride around. We'll look like two old people, one with a Q-tip for a head and you can just give everybody the queen's wave." We laughed in the back of the car. Cathy demonstrated her queen's wave—cupped hand, no arm flapping. We laughed in the back of that car and then went on to other subjects for the rest of the drive to the church.

Well, when we got to the church, an usher directed us to the pastor's office in the back. We were talking to the usher when the pastor came through the doors. It was right before we were going into the service.

"Brother Jesse," the pastor said, "I just have to do something."

I said, "What's that?"

"I want to show you something."

He led us to a garage that was just about ten feet away from his office. It was his parking spot at the church.

Inside that garage was a 2004 commemorative edition, cobalt-blue Corvette convertible.

My mouth dropped. We'd just seen a car almost exactly like it.

The pastor said, "I bought this two days ago, me and my wife, we love this car."

I immediately thought he wanted me to pray a blessing over it, so I got ready to pray.

But he didn't ask me to pray at all. Instead, he said, "The Lord told me it's not my car—it's yours."

I was shocked. I said, "What?"

"It's just got a hundred and fifty miles on it," he said, "This is yours." And he gave me the Corvette. I looked at that thing and I said, "Lord!!!" I looked at my watch. Forty-two minutes to the time that I said that I'd love to have one like it.

I heard the Lord speak to my spirit, "I heard you talk about it."

"Oh, Jesus!" I said.

The pastor asked, "Do you want to drive it home?"

I said, "No, no, I'll rent a truck and have them bring it home." I didn't want to put the miles on it!

I looked at that pastor and said, "Are you sure you want . . ."

He interrupted, "Yes, I can't help it. The Lord told me when I was driving it, 'This is not your car. This is Jesse Duplantis's car.'" I looked at Cathy, and she knew what I was thinking, *Look at what the Lord has done!*

I've never owned a Corvette in my life. I could have bought myself one, that's not the issue, but the Lord blessed me.

Well, we talked for a few moments more and it was time for church, time for me to preach the Gospel. We had a powerful meeting that night and many were blessed by the Word of the Lord.

Meanwhile, as Cathy and I flew back home that night, we were just in amazement of how good God is. I've got a sign that says, "God's been good to Jesse!" that I look at every time I'm traveling. I see those words, and it reminds me of how good God is, spiritually, physically, and financially. He blesses those who bless Him.

I'm reminded now of Psalm 84:11–12, where it says, *". . . no good thing will He withhold from them that walk uprightly. O LORD of hosts, blessed is the man that trusteth in Thee."*

Blessed is the man that trusts in God. It could also say, blessed is the man that has faith in God, that loves God, and puts His kingdom first! God is a rewarder of those that seek Him.

Notice that no good *thing* will He withhold from those that walk uprightly. That Corvette is a good thing to me. It's a sweet reminder of how God will give us the desires of our heart, if we delight ourselves in Him (Psalm 37:4).

Well, not long after that, the delivery truck showed up at my ministry. Cathy and I put the top down and we drove around New Orleans. I even leaned my seat back, like the young people do, and just enjoyed myself!

Sure, a cop stopped me one day . . . but that's just what I call obstacles! The cop looked at me. He knew who I was because he patrols my neighborhood.

"Brother Jesse, how you doing?"

"You like my Corvette?" I asked him.

He said, "I could barely see it when you went by me."

"The Lord gave me this!"

He looked at it and said, "You've got to be kidding me. If you don't slow down you're going to pay for it in tickets."

I said, "Yeah, but I've never had anything like this in my life!" He let me go, glory! The policeman understood that a blessing like that can cause a man to get excited, put his foot on the gas, glory to God. I may be old, but I'm not dead!

BUILDING MENTAL MAPS BRINGS BLESSING!

When I was on the way to that church in Chicago, I was building a mental map, not even realizing it. I was telling God, who lives within me, one of my desires. I have to tell you, I don't really have many desires outside of doing the work of God, but God heard that desire and he moved upon a man to fulfill it.

I have gotten to the point in my mental mapping that I have to watch out what I think about, because God will cause it to come to pass. I'm serious. I believe that this is what happens when you sow years of putting God first, when you open your mind to His limitless power and when you simply do what He's asked you to do. He is a rewarder of those that diligently seek Him.

Today, I'm fulfilling my divine destiny by being a minister of the Gospel. It wasn't something I thought I'd do, but it was God's plan, and it has become a true joy in my life.

PERSECUTION COMES WITH THE BLESSING

When God blesses you and you begin reaping the success of staying on the right track with God, don't expect everyone around you to be happy about it! The blessings of God sometimes come with persecution.

As a minister, I used to think that people would be happy to see God bless me and my family, but no! Many people knew my background. They knew what I had accomplished and what I gave up for the cause of Christ. But people didn't care what I gave up for God; they just didn't want me to prosper, no matter what. It bothered me until the Word showed me that blessing often comes "with persecution."

> And Jesus answered and said, "Verily I say unto you, There is no man that hath left house, or brethren, or sisters, or father, or mother, or wife, or children, or lands, for My sake, and the Gospel's.
> "But he shall receive an hundredfold **now in this time**, houses, and brethren, and sisters, and mothers, and children, and lands, **with persecutions;** and in the world to come eternal life."
>
> MARK 10:29–30

This showed me that those who believe God's Word and give up material things, relationships, and land for God or the sake of His Gospel will receive a hundredfold in this time—even houses and lands—but it *will* come with persecution.

It doesn't matter how many good things you've done or how much you've given up, some people simply enjoy attacking those who have honored God and are blessed. It's called jealousy—jealousy over your divine destiny as a prosperous believer.

Jealous people wonder, *Why don't I have what you have?* I give them one good reason, which they usually don't want to hear. They didn't want it enough to do what it takes to get it. They didn't want to build a mental map on the road to divine destiny.

WORK HARD, BELIEVE HARD

If you want anything in life, you've got to not just work hard, you have to *believe* hard! Plenty of people work hard and don't get much. They don't believe in themselves. They don't believe that they can go higher. So, even though they work and they see some increase, they don't go forward very much in joy.

If you want anything from God, you've got to believe in faith. You've got to put aside doubt, worry, fear, and anxiety in favor of faith and peace. Put faith and peace together, and you're going to be blessed. Again, in order to have true prosperity, the belief must come before hard work. Otherwise, you just end up with a lot of stuff and no peace! True prosperity encompasses the spiritual, physical, and financial parts of life, and it brings no sorrow with it.

Don't give up on God's plan for your life or God's blessings on your life just because somebody might criticize you. God is looking for somebody to take the persecution of being blessed, to get beyond what people think and start caring about what He thinks!

HIS PLAN IS YOUR DESTINY

God has a destiny for you that is just as important as mine. It's something that only you can do. What is it? Do you have a dream? Do you want to see it fulfilled?

God wants to see you have and enjoy this life. He just wants you to include Him in it. You know, in this book, we've talked about faith, about dreams, about the power of filling your mind with the Word and overcoming your weaknesses. But the very foundation of your success is going to depend on putting God first. He must be above everything in your life.

There is a Scripture in Luke 9:24 that I think is often misunderstood. There, Jesus says, *"For whosoever will save his life shall lose it: but whosoever will lose his life for My sake, the same shall save it."*

Some take this to mean that God doesn't ever want us to enjoy our life, but that's not true. He just wants it to be surrendered, fully, to Him. When you give your dreams to God, He will return them to you in ways you never thought possible.

My dream was once to play rock music. It was my path in life, the path I'd chosen. God had a destiny for me that was beyond what

I could think. It was beyond my talents. It was beyond my abilities, but it was His plan for my life.

I gave up my plan for His plan, and I'm so glad I did. He saved me not only from sin, but from myself. He wants to do the same for you.

Your destiny is greater than you think. It's found in losing yourself to Jesus, knowing that, with Him, you can only gain.

FOOTPRINTS TO VICTORY

God has left us His Word. It's like footprints that lead us on the road to our divine destiny, one victory at a time. When we simply follow the prints, we will be blessed! Blessed in the city! Blessed in the field! Blessed going in, and blessed going out! We'll be wiser, stronger, and better equipped to help others.

Don't accept just one area when it comes to the blessings of God. Let God be God over every area of your life, spiritually, physically, and financially—so that He can bless you in all those areas.

Sometimes life can render you hard and calloused. Experience can wear on you and make you give up hope—don't! Spend time with God, and let Him refresh you. Think of it like this: We may have lost a garden, but we've gained a Heaven. We may have gotten thrown out of the Garden of Eden, but bless God, we've got the New Jerusalem to look forward to now.

The devil lost it all when he went to war with God, and he is without hope. You are not. You have hope everlasting! The devil lost Heaven, and God has made you his boss—ha!! He's got to move when we use the name of Jesus and resist him. So, don't let the wear and tear of time make you calloused and hard to the things of God. Keep your heart soft, your sword of the Spirit sharp, and keep walking in His footsteps!

The devil is still out there roaming, seeking whom he may devour—don't let him devour your joy or your peace of mind. The mind is the first place he attacks, remember that.

WHAT ARE YOU BELIEVING FOR?

God is for you. He loves you. He wants to bless you, to give you not only a fulfilling life, but also the desires of your heart, whether that is to do something or to have something.

God is for you. He is never against you. When you put your faith in Him, you can expect that He will prove Himself to you as a faithful Father, a surprising Father!

God is not looking for ways to condemn you, hurt you, or make your path in life difficult. That's what the devil does. That's what a sin-sick earth brings.

Jesus died to redeem you from all sin. The Bible says you've been made FREE from the law of sin and death through the work of the cross. Jesus has washed you clean and God counts you righteous, which means that you can go through this life without guilt, without shame, and without limitation on your divine destiny. You are free. Don't let the devil, your thoughts, or anyone else steal that from you.

Your life doesn't have to be boring, short-lived, or poverty stricken. It can be long-lived and prosperous! You can fulfill God's plan for your life.

Why did Jesus come? So that we might LIVE! Jesus came to be our mediator to God and to restore us to our rightful place so that we could make Heaven our eternal home and live a good and truthful life on this earth, too. Jesus said, *"I am come that you might have life, and that they might have it more abundantly"* (John 10:10). The life that we've been given is a real gift. It's not been given to you to endure but to enjoy.

It's enjoyment to do what you're called to do. It's enjoyment to recognize the greatness of your own life, whether you've been called to do something simple or complex! All of us have our place in this world.

God knows that you are powerful. He knows that your words matter. He wants you to build a mental map on the road to your good destiny, to wake up in the morning with joy for the day.

You were destined to love people. You were destined to live by faith and not by sight. You were destined to bring truth and faith into the lives of other people. This is your part as a believer, as a member of the body of Christ.

This life is something that you are passing through. It's not the only life you'll live. Heaven awaits! It's a vapor according to James 4:14, but that doesn't mean that it's unimportant. This life can be good. You are going to do things here that you will remember and enjoy talking about for all of eternity in Heaven!

The years of your life pass by too quickly to just ignore your calling in life. You don't have to live miserably. You don't have to live bored. The Lord can fill you up with His presence, His joy, and His optimism for this life every day—and not just on Sunday! His Word is going to produce faith in you—faith that will help you to build a mental map on the road to your divine destiny.

AN OVERFLOW OF FAITH

Faith is what makes things happen in the spirit realm, and then in the natural world. When Jesus Christ walked this earth, He did miracles for those who believed, not for those who doubted.

Jesus not only walked on the water; He controlled the weather. When Jesus touched the lame man, he didn't just get up and walk. He leaped! He jumped!

When Jesus turned the water into wine, He didn't just make average-tasting stuff. It was the best. He didn't just make "just enough" wine; he made more than enough. He lived His life overflowing in faith. That's the kind of Christ we serve, and that's the kind of example we're supposed to follow in living out our lives.

Jesus's miracle of the two fishes and five loaves showed us that it was in His very nature to go beyond "just enough." There was "too much" miracle that day. The disciples picked up *twelve baskets* of fragments. That's a lot of leftovers! Do you think Jesus overshot that day? Maybe prayed too much? No, Jesus was just doing what

He said He came to do in John 10:10, to give life and that more *abundantly.*

Abundance is part of your destiny, but it isn't going to drop out of Heaven. It's going to come as you learn the Word and put your faith in it.

Joshua 1:8 NKJV says, *"This Book of the Law shall not depart from your mouth, but you shall meditate in it day and night, that you may observe to do according to all that is written in it. For then you will make your way prosperous, and then* **you** *will have good success."*

Notice that it doesn't say God is going to prosper you without you having a part in it. *You* will make your way prosperous. *You* will have good success. If you follow the Word, you will succeed. God will light your path. He will give you wisdom when you ask, guidance when you need it and, if you ask Him, He will give you new ideas and new concepts that will help you to fulfill your divine destiny.

MY LAST TWO TIPS

Years ago, while I was believing God for my dream of a television ministry to become reality, God taught me two things that became crucial to my success. The Lord said, "Jesse, I hate haughty eyes. Never say in your heart or with your mouth, 'Look what I have done.' If you do, the dream you're living now will stop, and the dream you're believing for will stop."

I found those very words in 2 Samuel 22:28, *". . . but thine eyes are upon the haughty, that thou mayest bring them down."* God hates pride. It's the root of what caused the devil to rebel, so when you act in pride, you're actually right at the center of rebellion.

Never forget "haughty eyes." God hates them, and pride will be your undoing, if you let it into your life. Proverbs 16:18 says, *"Pride goeth before destruction, and an haughty spirit before a fall."* This doesn't mean you should not be confident, but just be confident in God's ability to work through you. Never forget that if you think it's all you, then you're on the path to falling. You will lose what you desire unless you're committed to recognizing Him.

So, make sure you never have haughty eyes. Keep your humility, and you'll keep your success.

Next, God told me, "Because you're a giver, I'll open the windows for you. But if you want to dream like I dream, do this: Fulfill someone else's dream. Then yours will come to pass."

God showed me that fulfilling someone's dream before your own is all over the Bible. Joseph's dream couldn't be fulfilled until he fulfilled the butler's and baker's dreams. Jesus fulfilled the Father's dream and then Jesus's dream came true—His dream was *you*.

I started looking for dreams. I'd meet someone and ask, "Do you have a dream?"

"Yeah," they'd say, "God wants me to . . ."

"Let me fulfill your dream," I'd say, and I'd give to their dream or help them to do it.

"Oh, Jesse! What about your dream?"

"I want to fulfill yours, then God will take care of mine." And do you know what? As I fulfilled other people's dreams, God began to fulfill my own. I'd send someone to Bible School, and I'd suddenly be given a library of books. I'd send money to pay for cars at missions in third world countries, and suddenly I'd receive an unexpected deal on a car of my own. Whatever I "lost" to God never became a real sacrifice, because He always gave back to me, thirty, sixty, and a hundredfold. He still does it today.

As I pour out into other people's lives, He continues to pour out into mine. I preach to others, and the Word I speak also lifts me up. I lay my hands in the prayer of agreement for someone else's healing, and God also restores my body. This is the way God works. It's a life of giving, a destiny we all have to lose ourselves in God.

Do you have a dream today? Do you dream of fulfilling your destiny on earth? If so, sow your life into another's dream and God will honor yours. You will reap the fulfillment of all your dreams and more.

As you pursue Him, He will drop new dreams into your heart. He will give to you as you give to others. Lose yourself in God today. Put your faith toward something real. Build your mental map and just watch what God does for you . . . He will draw you out, build you up, and bring you right to the place where only *you* can go. Your divine destiny!

God bless you as you serve Him!

ACKNOWLEDGMENTS

To MY SON-IN-LAW, Eddie, who pushed me to get this book out and worked with everyone to see it completed; and to my daughter, Jodi, who helped me take my message and our conversations and turn them into this book—I love you both!

To David Epstein, who believed in me and my ministry from the beginning, and who led me to the wonderful Jan Miller.

To Jan Miller, Shannon Marven, Cheri Gillis, and the entire team Dupree, Miller & Associates for seeing the value in me and in this book: for signing me, guiding me through the process, and leading me to the great Simon & Schuster.

To Carolyn Reidy, Mark Gompertz, Chris Lloreda, and Sulay Hernandez at Simon & Schuster, for believing in me and in my message, being so supportive about the work, and so complimentary about the manuscript. Thank you for working so hard to reach so many. I know it takes a lot of people to get a book into the marketplace and I feel proud to be working with the best!

Thank you, I appreciate you all!